*As for me, may my prayer unto You,
O G-d, Be in a time of grace;*

*O G-d, in the abundance of Your mercy,
Answer me in the truth of Your Salvation.*

Psalm 69:14

ACKNOWLEDGMENTS

To my brother, Dov (Barry) Mindel, for his critical perusal of the manuscript.

To my wife, Nettie Mindel, for editorial assistance and proofreading.

To my daughter, Frida Schapiro, for preparing the Indexes.

To my young colleague, Rabbi Yosef Friedman, for technical assistance.

TABLE OF CONTENTS

Kabbalat Shabbat

Returning Home from Shul on Friday Eve

Kiddush for Shabbat

Shabbat Morning Prayers

The Shabbat Morning Amidah

vi

Prayers Before and After Reading From the Torah

Blessing the New Month

Musaf Amidah for Shabbat

Minchah for Shabbat

Havdalah

Indexes

FOREWORD

In 1972 the first volume of *As for Me, My Prayer* came off the press. Since then it was reprinted five times, the sixth printing appearing in 1984.

Considering, also, that the publication of that treatise and subsequent reprintings were not accompanied by fanfare advertising, it is fair to say that the popularity of the first volume of *My Prayer* has been very gratifying.

A further measure of the interest and demand which this work has generated may be found in the fact that it has been published also in Hebrew, French, Spanish and Russian editions.

We trust, therefore, that the present second volume of *My Prayer* will fare as well.

The nature and intent of this work is briefly explained in the *Preface* to the first volume, reproduced below; it is equally relevant to the present volume. Some additional remarks, however, are in order, with specific reference to the theme of this volume.

There is more than symbolism in ushering in the Shabbat with light — that of the Shabbat candles, and escorting it out with light — that of the braided Havdalah candle. In the language of the Kabbalah and Chassidut, light is identified with the first emanation from the Creator, *Or-Ein-Sof* ("Infinite Light").

One of the underlying principles of this metaphor is that physical light — radiation — has no independent existence. The moment it is separated from its source, it ceases to exist. The same is true of the entire created order, as well as of any particle of it, which is why creation is a *continuous* process. (This basic tenet is discussed more fully in Volume I, pp. 142f.).

A further significant point about light is that light itself is invisible; it becomes visible only when it is reflected from a material surface, be it even a speck of dust. A beam of sunlight can be seen slanting through a room only because it is glancing off dust particles in the air. The shafts of sunlight that are sometimes seen coming down through gaps in clouds are made visible by particles of haze or moisture present in the atmosphere. On the other hand, an astronaut suspended in outer space with the sun behind him, would see nothing; all is blackness (save the distant planets and stars). This is because the sun's rays would be streaming past him, with nothing to bounce them back to his eyes.

Light also has a transcending quality, illuminating all things indiscriminately, without itself being affected or soiled in the process.

Light has a number of additional remarkable attributes, the most essential one of which is that light is not a substance; it is energy.

The above mentioned (and unmentioned) characteristics of light make it a very apt metaphor, extensively used in Kabbalah and Chassidut literature, to help us understand in some measure the highly subtle and abstruse concepts relating to Creation, Divine Providence, the *Shechinah* (Divine Presence, both immanent and transcending), the significance of material objects in the performance of Mitzvot, and other related concepts, which the author had occasion to discuss at length elsewhere.[2]

Thus we can conceive of the Universe, as also of every thing in the created order, including inanimate objects, as consisting of a "body" and a "soul": The *body* comprising all aspects of a thing that can be perceived by our physical senses — corresponding to *reflected* physical light in the metaphor; while the spiritual aspects of a thing, those that cannot be perceived by the physical eye, but only by the "eye" of the intellect, would fall into the category of the *soul*, corresponding to the *direct* radiation flowing from its source of light — in the metaphor before us.

---

1. Nissan Mindel, *The Philosophy of Chabad*, 3rd printing, 1985. Kehot Publication Society, Brooklyn, N.Y. *The Commandments*, 9th ed. 1973, KPS.

The Shabbat, too, has a "body" and a "soul". The body comprises all the physical aspects of Shabbat — the candle lighting, the Shabbat meals and clothes, the special liturgy of the Shabbat prayers — all these sublimated components adding to the honor and delight of Shabbat. But the *soul* of Shabbat transcends all that; it is the hidden spiritual dimension of the total Shabbat experience; it has to be discovered and identified with in a personal way.

Nothing brings out this inner Shabbat soul more conceptually than the prayers of Shabbat. But in order to perceive this it is necessary to do more than just recite the words of the prayers; it is necessary to delve into the deeper meanings and concepts of the familiar words and phrases as they are illuminated by the sages of the Kabbalah and Chassidut.

The present volume is a modest attempt in this direction. The author has endeavored to bring out in some measure the taste and flavor of Shabbat through a deeper appreciation of the Shabbat prayers — at any rate in capsule form. Students with a more searching bent will find the footnotes helpful to get to the sources and pursue the topics more comprehensively. Indeed, in keeping with the dictum, "Give a little wisdom to the wise, and he (she) will gain a great deal of wisdom more" (Prov. 9:9), the effort will surely be rewarding.

Note: Although it is self-evident, it should be noted that the present volume discusses only prayers that are recited on Shabbat (some of which on Yom Tov, too). Prayers that are recited also on weekdays are discussed in Volume I.

NISSAN MINDEL

Nissan, 5749.

PREFACE
(To Volume One)

The present volume is not a translation of the *Siddur*, but rather a commentary and an exposition. Quotations and excerpts from the prayers, in their English rendition, are presented primarily for the purpose of spotlighting the main themes, ideas, and concepts contained in the prayers. In such instances the author frequently chose to render his own translation where he felt that his version would more accurately reflect the thoughts behind the text.

Our daily prayers consist almost entirely of selections and readings from our sacred literature, the T'NaCh (our Holy Bible) and the Talmud. The selection and order (hence, "Siddur") of these prayers are the creation of our Divinely inspired Prophets and Sages. Thus our prayers echo the eternal and infinite word of G-d. We address ourselves to G-d in *His own words*, inasmuch as human language is too poor and too limited to convey the sublime outpouring of our Divine soul — for this is the essential meaning of *Tefilah*, "service of the heart," as explained more fully in the Introduction.

In arranging the structure of our daily prayers, our Prophets and Sages of old were mindful to select Biblical and Talmudic passages which would evoke our deepest religious feelings and inspire our soulful attachment to our Father in Heaven. But, at the same time, they were equally mindful to include texts which contain the basic truths and tenets of our faith, from elementary moral and ethical values to the highest concept of pure Monotheism which we proclaim in the *Shema*. They clearly intended the Siddur to be both inspirational and instructive. To put it in another way, our Siddur was designed to be not only the vehicle for the "service of the heart" but also to be a vehicle for the "service of the mind." This is where *kavanah* — attunement of both the heart and the mind — comes in. Indeed, it has been said that *kavanah* is the very soul of prayer, and that "prayer without *kavanah* is like a body without a soul."

Unfortunately, human nature is such that the repetition of the prayers day after day, some sections of it three times daily, tends to reduce what should be a profound daily experience to an absent-minded recitation. To be sure, even a superficial recital of the daily prayers has value, since it cannot be devoid of an awareness of G-d and of a sense of dependence on Him. However, in order that our prayers should impress themselves upon our heart and mind, a basic knowledge, at least, of their *inner* meaning and content is indispensable.

This, then, is the main purpose of the present commentary: To bring out and expound the deeper content of our daily prayers.

Hopefully, the reader who takes time out to read through the following pages will find his knowledge of our daily prayers enriched in some measure, and his appreciation of the Siddur deepened in some degree. If so, his effort, and the author's, will be amply rewarded.

NISSAN MINDEL

Nissan, 5732
Long Beach, N.Y.

THE UNIQUE NATURE OF SHABBAT

Introduction to the Shabbat Prayers

In order to obtain a deeper insight into the prayers of Shabbat, it is well to get more closely acquainted with Shabbat itself. What is the special nature of this day? What does the Shabbat mean to us, and what is its universal message?

We shall, therefore, dwell briefly on the main aspects of Shabbat, particularly those that are reflected in the Shabbat prayers.

I. The Shabbat Bride

The Torah tells us, in the beginning, that G-d created the world in six days, and that by the end of the sixth day the heaven and earth and all their hosts were completed. Then G-d rested from all creative activity, "and G-d blessed the seventh day and made it holy."[1]

Thus, right from the beginning of Creation, G-d has set the Shabbat day apart from the other days of the week, as a *holy* day.

But for whom was the Shabbat meant? Who was to accept it, appreciate it and keep it holy? The answer is to be found in the following meaningful Midrash:

> *Rabbi Shimon ben Yochai taught: When G-d created the holy Shabbat, it said to the Holy One, blessed be He: "Every day You created has a mate. Am I to be the only odd one, without a mate?" Replied G-d, "The Jewish people will be your mate." And so, while the Jewish*

---

1. Genesis 2:1-3.

1

*people stood at the foot of Mount Sinai to receive the
Torah and become a nation, G-d declared (in the Ten
Commandments): "Remember the Shabbat day to keep
it holy!" As if to say, "Remember My promise to the
Shabbat that the Jewish nation shall be its mate."*[2]

The Holy *Zohar*[3] speaks of the Jewish people and the Shabbat
in terms of bridegroom and bride, and this is why the Shabbat is
welcomed with the words, *Bo'i kallah, bo'i kallah* — "Welcome,
bride; welcome, bride!"[4] The repetition, *bo'i kallah,* alludes to
the two great qualities of the "bride," being both "blessed" and
"holy," as it is written, "And G-d blessed the seventh day and
made it holy."[5] Indeed, according to Rabbi Yitzchak Arama in
his *Akedat Yitzchak,*[6] the word *l'kadsho* — "to keep it holy" —
may be rendered "to betroth it," in the sense of *kiddushin.*

In this way our Sages tell us that the Shabbat is uniquely
Jewish, that is to say, that the Jewish people and the Shabbat are
inseparable; they were destined for each other from the moment
of their "birth." Without the Shabbat the Jewish people is
simply unthinkable, just as without the Torah the Jewish people
is unthinkable. This is one of the reasons why the Shabbat was
equated with all the Mitzvot of the Torah.[7]

II. Shabbat of Creation

As mentioned earlier, the origin of the Shabbat, referred to as
Shabbat of Creation, is given in the section of *Vayechulu,*[8] which
is included in the first *Amidah* (*Arvit*) of Shabbat. Shabbat is not
mentioned again explicitly in the Torah until after the story of

2. *Bereshit Rabbah* 11:9.
3. *Tikkunei Zohar* 69a.
4. *Bavli, Shabbat* 119a.
5. Genesis 2:3.
6. *Bereshit, Shaar* 4.
7. *Yerushalmi.* Ber. ch. 1:5; *Shemot Rabbah* 25:16.
8. Gen. 2:1-3.

the Exodus (*Yetziat Mitzraim*), in connection with the manna. This heavenly bread did not come down on the Shabbat but, instead, the children of Israel received a double portion on Friday for Shabbat as well. Then Mosheh Rabbeinu told the children of Israel: "See, G-d has given you this Shabbat."[9] The Shabbat was nothing new for the children of Israel, for, as our Sages tell us, they had known about it traditionally from the time of Abraham and, indeed, observed it even in Egypt. But on this occasion they received the first laws about Shabbat, and several weeks later they received formal instructions on Shabbat in the Ten Commandments at Mount Sinai.[10]

After the Torah was given to our people, the commandment to observe the Shabbat is repeated in the Torah many times with great emphasis. One of the better known passages about the Shabbat is included in the Morning *Amidah*:

> *And the children of Israel shall keep the Shabbat... as an everlasting covenant. It is a sign between Me and the children of Israel forever: That in six days G-d made heaven and earth, and on the seventh day He ceased from work and rested.*[11]

Here the Torah tells us of the basic significance of the Shabbat as the living sign of G-d's creation. By keeping the Shabbat, we, the Jewish people, proclaim aloud that G-d is the Creator of heaven and earth, and we reaffirm the everlasting covenant between G-d and the Jewish people. G-d has crowned His creation with the Shabbat, and has given this crown to us. Our Sages of the Talmud expressed it this way: "A precious gift — says G-d — have I in My treasure stores; its name is Shabbat, and I have given it to you."[12]

Wearing this crown is, of course, a great privilege: it makes us

---

9. Exodus 16:29.
10. Exodus 20:8 ff.
11. Ibid. 31:16-17.
12. Shabbat 10b.

G-d's witnesses on earth. But it also places upon us great respon-
sibilities. These are summed up by Maimonides as follows:

> The Shabbat and the prohibition of idolatry are each
> weighted against the rest of the commandments of the
> Torah. The Shabbat is the everlasting sign between G-d
> and the people of Israel. Therefore, the Jew who dese-
> crates any of the other commandments is regarded as a
> transgressor, while he who publicly desecrates the Shab-
> bat is considered as a heathen (denying the existence of
> G-d). He who observes the Shabbat properly, honoring
> it and delighting in it to the best of his ability, is given a
> reward in this world, over and above the reward that is
> reserved for him in the World To Come. [13]

More than anything else, it has been the Shabbat that has
distinguished the Jewish people from all other nations of the
world throughout the ages to this day. For this was not just a
matter of a single precept, or custom, but something that is
fundamental to the Jewish religion and Jewish way of life. An
entire day of the week (actually 26 hours) is set apart, during
which the Jew not only desists from work, closes down stores,
factories, workshops and halts all work at home — but is completely transformed into a person of holiness, devoting the time
to prayer and study. Even *externally* this transformation is in
evidence — in one's dress, eating, walking and talking. For
thousands of years the nations of the world could not understand this Jewish Shabbat. They, who had not known a rest day
in the week altogether, thought it deplorable for an entire nation
to take off a whole day in the week. When Haman complained
to King Ahasuerus about the "one people, scattered and
dispersed among the nations, whose laws are different from
those of any other nation,"[14] it was Shabbat and the festivals
that he held up to ridicule.[15] Ancient Roman historians called

---

13. Rambam Code, *Zemanim Hilchot* Shabbat 30.
14. Esther 3:8.
15. Esther *Rabbah* 7:14.

the Jewish people "lazy" and "uncivilized" for their adherence to the Shabbat. When the nations of the world finally recognized the Torah as a holy book, and called it "The Book" (Bible), they adopted some of its principles. They also introduced a "Sabbath" or "day of rest" into their religions. But it is significant that they made it on Sunday (in Christianity), or on Friday (in Islam). The Shabbat remained Jewish for Jews alone! One can clearly see the Hand of Divine Providence in this. Although "imitation is the highest form of flattery," nothing in the imitations can approach the original, Divinely ordained, holy Shabbat, as anyone familiar with the laws of Shabbat and their significance knows.

III. Remembrance of Yetziat Mitzraim

In the Kiddush recited on Friday night, we thank HaShem for giving us the Shabbat "as a memorial to the work of Creation (זכרון למעשה בראשית)" and also "as a remembrance of the Exodus from Egypt (זכר ליציאת מצרים)."

These two basic perceptions of Shabbat are derived from the Ten Commandments, the fourth of which deals with Shabbat. In the first Decalogue it is stated: "Remember the Shabbat day ...for in six days HaShem made heaven and earth, the sea and all that is in them, and ceased work on the seventh day; wherefore HaShem blessed the Shabbat day and sanctified it."[16] The text in the second Decalogue reads: "Observe the Shabbat day to keep it holy.... And you shall remember that you were a slave in the land of Egypt, and HaShem your G-d brought you out of there by a mighty hand and by an outstretched arm; therefore HaShem your G-d commanded you to keep the Shabbat day."[17]

Commenting on the different aspects of Shabbat as reflected in the Ten Commandments in Exodus and Deuteronomy respec-

---

16. Exodus 20:8-11.
17. Deuteronomy 5:12-15.

tively, the *Ramban* (Nachmanides) explains that, far from being contradictory, they are supportive and complementary. For as the day of rest attesting to the Creation, Shabbat also brings to mind the time when the Jewish people, being enslaved in Egypt, were not free to rest on that day; they had to work on all seven days of the week. Hence the Torah emphasizes, "in order that your man-servant and your maid-servant may rest as well as you."[18]

In a deeper sense, the *Ramban* continues, the Exodus from Egypt confirmed and deepened our belief without doubt in HaShem as Creator of the universe.

Until *Yetziat Mitzraim*, the belief in One G-d came down to the Jewish people from Abraham, Isaac and Jacob, the founders of our Jewish nation, along with the unique covenant that had been established between HaShem and the Patriarchs and their descendants. During the centuries of enslavement, however, belief and tradition were put to severe test. Many, if not most, of the enslaved Jews must have had some doubts whether there really was a Supreme Being, Creator and Master of the world, or if such a Being had not abandoned the world to its devices, or to the mighty Pharaohs.

Yetziat Mitzraim, with all its wonders and miracles, demonstrated without any doubt that G-d was truly the Creator and Master of the world, since He was able at will to suspend and change the laws of nature.

Moreover, *Yetziat Mitzraim* demonstrated, too, that Divine *Hashgachah* ("watchfulness," Providence) extends to every particular and detail of the created order, to humans as well as to the lower orders of animal and plant life, even to the inanimate.

A third essential element of the Exodus experience was the revelation of prophecy. It established the fact that the Creator not only bestowed upon Mosheh the gift of prophecy, but made him the greatest of all prophets (forty-eight men and seven

---

18. Exodus 20:10.

women, according to our Sages[19]). It was at the miraculous
crossing of *Yam Suf* ("Reed Sea") that the liberated Israelites
attained complete "trust in G-d and in Mosheh His servant"[20]
— meaning, "in the *prophecy* of Mosheh His servant."[21] This
absolute belief in the truth of Mosheh's prophecy is no less a
cornerstone of our Jewish faith than the belief in the two fundamental principles mentioned above, namely, the existence of a
Supreme Being as Creator of the world, and Divine Providence
extending to the smallest detail of the created order. For,
although the entire nation witnessed the Divine Revelation at
Mount Sinai and heard the Decalogue, the *entire* Torah with all
its 613 Mitzvot was transmitted through Mosheh; as G-d's true
prophet, he served as G-d's "mouthpiece," and his testimony
had the same authority and force as if heard directly from G-d
Himself.

In light of the above, the *Ramban* points out, we can appreciate the Talmudic declaration that "Shabbat equibalances all
the Mitzvot,"[22] since by keeping Shabbat we attest to the truth
of all the fundamental principles of our faith: Creation *ex nihilo*,
Divine Providence and Divine Prophecy.

Thus, *Ramban* concludes, Shabbat is a remembrance of *Yetziat Mitzraim,* while *Yetziat Mitzraim,* in turn, is a memorial to
Shabbat of Creation.[23]

IV. To Make the Shabbat

Referring to the above-mentioned verse, "And the children of
Israel shall keep (*v'shamru*) the Shabbat, to make (*la'asot*) the

---

19. *Megillah* 14a.
20. Exodus 14:31.
21. *Onkelos,* ibid.
22. *Yerushalmi Berachot* 1:15, *Bavli Nedarim,* end ch. 3; *Shemot
    Rabbah* 25:16.
23. Ramban on Deuteronomy 5:15.

Shabbat," etc., our Sages declare that *v'shamru* refers to all the laws pertaining to the cessation of work and all that we may not do on Shabbat; *la'asot* refers to all things that we have to put into the Shabbat, to honor it, delight in it and fill it with holiness through prayer and study.[24] *Jews make the Shabbat, and Shabbat makes the Jewish people.* That is what is meant by referring to the Shabbat and the Jewish people as real mates, as mentioned earlier. Indeed, more than the Jewish people kept the Shabbat, the Shabbat has kept the Jewish people, for more than anything else the Shabbat unites all Jews, in all parts of the world. The Jewish people have always been a minority among the nations of the world, and most of the time surrounded by a hostile world. But through the observance of the Shabbat, the Jewish people partake from the infinite strength of the Creator: like the Shabbat itself which is "blessed" and "holy," the Jewish people keeping the Shabbat are blessed and holy, and remain under the direct protection of G-d Himself.

While the Shabbat and the Jewish people were designated from the time of Creation as inseparable "mates," and the Shabbat has remained uniquely Jewish, its universal message for all mankind is as relevant today as it has ever been. It proclaims, as noted above, the sovereignty of the Creator, His constant watchfulness (*Hashgachah*), and the authenticity of the Torah, the three most fundamental truths that the Jewish people constantly reaffirm by keeping the Shabbat holy, as Nachmanides emphasizes.

This Torah also incorporates the so-called Noahide Laws — the seven basic moral laws, with all their ramifications, that G-d ordained for the descendants of Noah (i.e., all mankind). These Divinely ordained moral laws must form the foundation of every human society, if it is to be truly human. No man-made legislature, however supportive, can supplant these *Divinely ordained* moral laws, since man-made laws are, by their very nature, sub-

---

24. *Shabbat* 218a/b; cf. Rambam Code, *Hilchot* Shabbat 30.

ject to change, abrogation and evasion, as human experience through the ages so woefully attests.

The Shabbat is, therefore, a reminder to all mankind that it must persistently move toward the "day that is all Shabbat" — a world where *all* the nations of the world will recognize the sovereignty of the Creator and His rule on earth, a world in which there is no strife, nor violence, nor injustice, for the spirit of Shabbat-peace will permeate the whole world.

There is the assurance of the Torah that eventually "the day that is all Shabbat" will most certainly become a reality.

סדר קבלת שבת
KABBALAT SHABBAT

Introductory Psalms

The Friday evening service, *Kabbalat Shabbat* ("Welcoming the Shabbat"), begins with six psalms: 95-99 and 29. The custom of reciting these psalms is relatively new. In ancient days, to be sure, the Shabbat was also welcomed in a special way just before sunset. From the Talmud we learn, for example, that Rabbi Chanina used to put on his best clothes and say, "Come, let us go forth and welcome the Shabbat Queen."[1] No doubt some appropriate psalms were recited on this occasion. The custom of beginning the service with the six psalms mentioned above, followed by the hymn of *Lecha Dodi*, however, is actually only about 400 years old. It was introduced by the great Kabbalist Rabbi Mosheh Cordovero (1522-1570) of Safed (brother-in-law of Rabbi Shlomo Halevi Alkabetz, author of *Lecha Dodi*), and has been held by both Sefardi and Ashkenazi Jews ever since.

The six psalms represent the Six Days of Creation which preceded the holy Shabbat day of rest.[2] They are hymns of praise to G-d, which serve to inspire us and put us in the right frame of mind for welcoming the Shabbat Queen. It has been noted that the *Rashei tevot* (the first letters of the initial words) of these psalms add up to 430, the numerical value of the Hebrew word נפש (soul), significant of the soulful inspiration that these psalms bring us on the eve of Shabbat.[3]

---

1. *Shabbat* 119a.
2. According to R.M. Cordovero, as quoted in Siddur *Otzar Hatefilot*, vol. I, p. 590.
3. Ibid.

Taking a closer look at these psalms, we can distinguish three
main themes that run through all of them.

One is the spirit of joy and exultation that permeates these
psalms. It sets our mood for our welcoming the Shabbat with
true joy, as one of the greatest gifts that G-d gave the people.

The second theme that is common to all these psalms is that of
Creation, for Shabbat is the "crown" of G-d's creative work.
This theme calls forth in us our acknowledgment of G-d's
majesty and our willing submission to His kingship. Many verses
in these psalms express such sentiments in various ways.

The third theme is the anticipation of the Messianic Era and
the new order that will transform this world into what is generally called *Olam haBa*, the World to Come; at that time our
material world will attain the ultimate perfection for which it is
destined and G-d's supreme majesty will be acknowledged by *all*
the nations of the world. That new world is due to become a
reality in the *seventh* millennium, which is appropriately called
"Shabbat." The preceding six thousand years of mankind's history compare to the six days of the week in relation to Shabbat.
This is particularly true of the present millennium (the sixth). It
is like "*Erev* Shabbat," the eve of Shabbat, when the final preparations for Shabbat must be made. With this in mind, our Sages
observed, "He who prepares for Shabbat on *Erev* Shabbat, has
food for Shabbat, but he who does not prepare for Shabbat,
what will he eat on Shabbat?"[4] The "food" they speak of is the
Torah and Mitzvot, the real food of our souls. This is the time to
prepare ourselves for the period that is called the "Eternal Shabbat," through the most dedicated adherence to the Torah and
Mitzvot in daily life, so to enjoy fully the great rewards of the
Eternal Shabbat. Indeed, Shabbat itself has some of the quality
of *Olam haBa*.[5]

---

4. *Avodah Zarah* 3a; *Kohelet Rabbah* 4:8; *Ruth Rabbah* 3:3; *Pirkei
   d'Rabbi Eliezer* 43.
5. *Berachot* 57b.

With the above in view, we will now take a closer look, however briefly, at each of the six psalms.

לכו נרננה
Psalm 95: Lechu Neran'na

The opening verses of this psalm are:

> *Come, let us sing unto G-d,*
> *Let us chant in joy to the Rock of our salvation...*
> *In whose hands are the depths of the earth,*
> *And the heights of the mountains are His.*
> *His is the sea, it is He who made it,*
> *And His hand formed the dry land....*

The next verse is especially significant, for, according to our
Sages, these very words were the first to be uttered by Adam,
immediately after G-d had breathed the spirit of life into his
body:

> *Come, let us bow down and kneel,*
> *Let us bend the knee before G-d, our Maker.*

This was the call that Adam, the first man created by G-d
Himself, addressed to all the creatures of the world: To acknowledge the kingship of G-d, the Creator, and to submit to His will
completely.[6]

We, as Jews, have reason to be even more responsive to this
call,

> *For He is our G-d, and we are the people of His pasture,*
> *the flock guided by His hand — this day, if you will only*
> *hearken to His voice.*

How aptly does this express the special relationship between
G-d and our people: He is our Shepherd, and we are His own

---

6. *Pirkei d'Rabbi Eliezer* 11; *Zohar* I, Vayechi 221b, etc.

flock; we are directly under His Divine Providence. It is, therefore, our special duty to hearken to His voice and carry out His
commandments — *this day,* meaning, *in this world* (Rashi), in
this world of action.

Having expressed this special relationship between G-d and
the Jewish people as Shepherd and flock, the psalmist goes on to
refer to the Exodus of our people from Egypt and the forty
years' wandering through the desert. That was the time when
G-d first showed His personal concern for our people and the
special care He took of His flock. The psalm concludes on a note
of caution: The "resting place," the Promised Land, can be
reached only by following the way of G-d — *if you will only
hearken to His voice.*

שירו לה'
Psalm 96: Shiru L'Hashem

This psalm, too, begins with a rousing call to sing G-d's
praises:

> *Sing unto G-d a new song*
> *Sing unto God all the earth!*

The psalm speaks of the Messianic Era, when the extraordinary salvation that G-d will have brought to our people will call
for a new kind of praise, a "new song." G-d's glory will be seen
also by the nations of the world, and the Psalmist calls upon us
to:

> *Declare His glory among the nations,*
> *His wonder among all peoples.*

The revelation of G-d's majesty and power in those future
days will cause all mankind to worship G-d with a sense of
holiness and trembling:

> *Worship G-d in beauty of holiness,*
> *Tremble before Him, all the earth.*

The whole of Nature will join in a chorus of praises to G-d:

The heavens will be glad and the earth will rejoice,
The ocean will roar and the fullness of it;
The field will rejoice and all that is therein
Then will all the trees of the forest sing with joy.

The "field" is a metaphor for this world, and "all that is therein" are all the creatures. "Trees" are often used as symbols of men. Jews are likened to fruit-bearing trees, because they constantly produce the fruits of Mitzvot and good deeds. But in the future, even the "trees of the forest," trees that bore no fruits, will rejoice, for everybody will produce good fruits.

The last verse of this psalm is an echo of the first, directly referring to the new world order, when G-d will dispense justice in the world:

Before G-d, Who comes, yea, He comes to judge the earth;
He will judge the world with righteousness, and nations with equity.

ה׳ מלך
Psalm 97: HaShem Malach

G-d reigns, the earth will be glad,
Many isles will rejoice...

This psalm is a continuation of the preceding one (especially verse 10). It speaks of the future, of the Messianic Era, when G-d will demonstrate His kingship over the whole earth, including the distant isles. It will be an occasion for tremendous rejoicing, for the world will then enter the era of its fulfillment and perfection.

Cloud and thick darkness are about Him,
Righteousness and justice are the foundations of His throne.

While G-d Himself will still be hidden from man, as if He were surrounded by a cloud and by darkness — for the essence of G-d cannot be grasped by the human intellect. Nevertheless, His reign on earth will be clearly recognized by His dispensing righteousness and justice. The first act of Divine justice will be the destruction of His enemies:

A fire will go before Him
And will consume His enemies around.

According to Rashi, this refers to Gog and Magog (leading the enemies of G-d and of the Jews) who, after overpowering many nations, will gather their forces against the Jews, and will be utterly destroyed by an earthquake, pestilence, fire and brimstone, and mutual slaughter, as prophesied by Ezekiel:[7] that will be the time, as the Psalmist goes on, when "all idol-worshipers will be put to shame," and "all gods will lie prostrate before the L-rd of all the earth." And:

Zion heard and rejoiced
And the cities of Judah were glad,
Because of Your judgments, O G-d.
For it is You, O G-d, Who are supreme over all the
earth,
You are most exalted over all gods.

The Psalmist therefore calls upon "those who love G-d to hate evil" — *now,* and not wait for the time when G-d will banish it. One who truly loves G-d cannot be indifferent to evil; the strength of one's love for G-d can be measured by the intensity of one's hatred of evil. However, it is evil itself, not the evil-doer, that the lover of G-d is called upon to hate. For very often the evil-doer acts out of ignorance or for other reasons, and in such cases he should be pitied and helped. But if there are really wicked men who might oppose any attempt to eradicate evil, the pious man need not fear them, for the Psalmist assures us:

---

7. Ezekiel chs. 38 and 39.

G-d preserves the souls of His pious ones,
He rescues them from the hand of the wicked.

The righteous will surely triumph in the end, as the psalm concludes:

Light is sown for the righteous
And for the upright of heart — rejoicing.
Rejoice, O ye righteous, in G-d
And give praise at the remembrance of His holiness.

"Light is sown for the righteous" (*or zarua latzadik*) — these are meaningful words. The good works that a person does are likened to the sowing or planting of seeds. The analogy brings out several significant facts. A seed (of a fruit-tree, for example) planted in the soil eventually produces a fruit-bearing tree. The results are extraordinary, for the seed is very small, and it has no taste or fragrance, yet out of it grows a huge tree with delicious fruits. The reward of sowing and planting is by far greater than the effort. All this we find also in the case of doing a Mitzvah. "The Mitzvot were not given for enjoyment," our Sages declare.[8] We do a Mitzvah because G-d commanded us to do it, whether we understand it or not. But the reward is sure to be enjoyable and delicious, and infinitely greater than the small effort or little sacrifice involved. Furthermore, it takes time for the seed to grow into a fruit-bearing tree; so also in the case of a Mitzvah. We must not expect an immediate reward, for the main reward is to come in the future world, *Olam haBa.* But G-d may be relied upon to keep His promise, and the Psalmist therefore calls: "Rejoice, ye righteous, in G-d."

The "light" sown for the righteous refers, of course, to Torah and Mitzvot, "for a Mitzvah is a lamp and the Torah is light."[9] The Midrash states that G-d planted the Torah and Mitzvot here on earth (instead of giving them to the angels in heaven) in order to enable us to inherit the World to Come. In His goodness, G-d

---

8. *Rosh Hashanah* 28a.
9. Proverbs 6:23.

left no thing or place in this world where He did not plant
Mitzvot: in the field — there are many Mitzvot connected with
every activity of plowing, sowing, reaping and so forth; in the
home — there is the Mezuzah; in clothing — *tzitzit* and *shatnes.*
And so at every step throughout his life, a Jew has many opportunities to do Mitzvot.[10] Because the Torah and Mitzvot are
G-d's wisdom and will, they are infinite, just as G-d Himself is
infinite. This is why, when a Jew studies G-d's Torah and
observes G-d's commandments, he sows something that contains the seeds that produce *infinite* results and *infinite* fruits and
rewards beyond our limited understanding and imagination. We
can only rejoice in the thought that G-d has chosen us to do His
Mitzvot, and in this way made it possible for us to share in His
holiness. It is therefore only right, as the Psalmist concludes, that
we should "give praise at the remembrance of His holiness."

מזמור שירו
Psalm 98: Mizmor, Shiru

A Psalm, Sing unto G-d a new song,
For He has done wonders...

Like the previous psalms, Psalm 98 also speaks of the Messianic Era. It is especially similar to Psalm 96, beginning and
ending with almost identical verses.

Here, too, the Psalmist acclaims G-d's pending wondrous acts
when the time comes to reveal His might and glory ("His right
hand and holy arm"). The poet speaks in the past tense, as if he
already saw it happen —

G-d has made known His saving power,
Before the eyes of the nations He has revealed His
righteousness.

---

10. *Bamidbar Rabbah, Shelach* 17:7.

During the long and dark *galut* (exile) the nations of the world mocked and derided the Jewish people, saying that G-d had forgotten and forsaken them, and they could therefore be oppressed and persecuted without fear of punishment. But those wicked nations are due to find out how wrong they were, as the psalm continues:

> *He remembered His mercy and faithfulness to the House of Israel;*
> *All (dwellers of) earth's farthest ends have seen the saving power of our G-d.*

Inspired by this wonderful vision of the ultimate triumph of the Jewish people and of the new revelation of G-d's glory on earth, the Psalmist calls for shouts of joy and songs of praise to G-d:

> *Sing praises to G-d with the harp,*
> *With the harp and the voice of praise;*
> *With trumpets and sound of the Shofar*
> *Proclaim (sovereignty) before the King, G-d.*

As often before, the Psalmist visualizes the whole of nature joining in the chorus of praise to G-d:

> *The sea and its fullness will thunder praise,*
> *The world and all who dwell therein;*
> *Rivers will clap hands,*
> *Together, mountains will sing joyously —*
> *Before G-d; for He comes to judge the earth.*
> *He will judge the earth with righteousness,*
> *And the nations with equity.*

ה׳ מלך

Psalm 99: HaShem Malach

> *G-d reigns, the nations will tremble:*
> *He Who dwells (reigns) above the cherubim — the earth will quake.*

Continuing the theme of the preceding psalm, the Psalmist declares that when G-d reveals His reign on earth, the nations of the world will tremble with fear of the Divine Judgment awaiting them.

"He Who dwells above the cherubim"[11] refers to the Divine Presence (the *Shechinah*) which, in the time of the *Bet Hamikdash*, was especially evident in the Holy of Holies. It was there that the Holy Ark (containing the Tablets with the Ten Commandments) reposed, its cover (*kapporet*) having two winged figures of cherubim with faces of children hammered out of gold, shielding the *kapporet*. It was from there that G-d's voice went out to Mosheh *Rabbeinu*.[12]

> *G-d is great in Tzion.*
> *And high is He above all the nations.*

According to Rashi, this refers to the battle of Gog and Magog, the mighty powers that will make their final attempt to destroy the Land of Israel, but will suffer a miraculous defeat on the mountains of Zion (Jerusalem), in accordance with the prophecy of Yecheskel.[13] Then

> *They will praise His name: It is great and awesome; holy is He.*
> *And the might of the King is loving justice.*
> *You established equity; justice and righteousness in Jacob — You ordained.*

The above lines are particularly meaningful.

To begin with, when the Torah speaks of G-d's "Name," it should be understood in a similar sense to that of a person's name; the name is not the person himself, but something by which he is identified. When we hear a familiar name, we immediately recall a familiar person: his face, appearance, voice and

---

11. See also Psalms 80:2.
12. Exodus 25:22.
13. Ezekiel chs. 38 and 39.

all that we know about that person and his conduct. But all these things are really *external* characteristics, as we perceive them with our senses; they do not tell us much about the person's *inner* soul and its *hidden* qualities.

In a similar way, when the Torah speaks of G-d's "Name," it speaks about the Divine qualities ("attributes") by which G-d makes Himself known to us, His creatures. This is all that we can know about G-d. In other words, we can know something about G-d from His works, but we cannot know G-d Himself. Or, to put it in another way: we can know what G-d *does,* but not what G-d *is.*

This, then, is the meaning of such expressions as G-d is "great, awesome, holy," and the like. They all speak of G-d's powers which are revealed to us through His works, which are great, awesome, holy and so forth.

But we must bear in mind that even to know G-d from His works is not a simple matter. A man's works can be seen almost at a glance, but G-d's works are timeless, where the past, present and future merge into one moment. For, man's lifespan — even if a person lives to 120 years — is very short compared with the eternity of the soul, which has life also before and after its lifespan on earth. No one but G-d knows what happened to it before, and what will happen to it later. Thus it is written, "For a thousand years is in Your eyes but like yesterday."[14] This statement also is only in a manner of speaking, or, as our Sages tell us, "the Torah speaks in the language of man." It is meant to give us *some* idea about the difference between what time is to us, and what it is to G-d. It is also meant to tell us that better than we can know what happened yesterday, G-d knows everything that happened in a thousand years (and countless thousands) in the past, or will happen in the future. It further reminds us that our knowledge is not like G-d's knowledge. For, a human being, even the wisest, can know, more or less, what

---

14. Psalms 90:4.

happened yesterday, but he cannot know what will happen tomorrow. But for G-d, yesterday, today and tomorrow are all the same. This is why we cannot properly understand G-d's works and G-d's ways, as the prophet has already cautioned us: "For My thoughts are not like your thoughts, and My ways are not like your ways, says G-d."[15]

With the above in mind we can better understand what is meant by the words, G-d's Name is "great and awesome."

G-d's Name is "great" in the sense that He can extend His benevolent powers endlessly; G-d's Name is "awesome" (inspiring awe and fear) in the sense that He can withhold and "contract" His powers endlessly. These two Divine attributes are generally termed *chesed* ("kindness") and *gevurah* ("might"), respectively. G-d applies these two powers both in the act of Creation as well as in His Divine Providence. The creation of the world is, first of all, an act of Divine benevolence *(chesed)*, since He did not have to create the world for His benefit, but is purely for the benefit of His creatures. So it is written, "The world was created (through) *chesed.*"[16] However, since it is G-d's plan to have a *material* world, limited in time and space (the last and lowest in a series of many spiritual worlds), G-d applied in Creation also the attribute of *gevurah* in order to limit and withhold His infinite powers. As a result, we live in a world where G-d's powers and "presence" are both revealed and hidden. It can be seen, however, that G-d's attribute of *gevurah* is really also an act of *chesed,* since without *gevurah* the world as we know it could not come into existence. In other words, the quality of *gevurah* is hidden in that of *chesed,* or, to put it more simply, it is *chesed* in disguise.

Similarly, *chesed* and *gevurah* come into play in Divine Providence, that is, how G-d cares and provides for His creatures to the minutest detail. Sometimes G-d's kindness and benevolence

15. Isaiah 55:8.
16. Psalms 89:3.

are evident on the surface, but more often they are concealed, for only G-d really knows how much good needs to be revealed to a particular person. Thus, there are times when G-d's attribute of *chesed* gives way to His attribute of *gevurah,* and a person finds that things seem to go wrong. But, as already noted, *gevurah* is *chesed* in disguise, and G-d surely knows how much of His *gevurah* a person can take to bring him just the right measure of benefit.

This interplay of *chesed* and *gevurah* in Divine Providence can be easily illustrated by the manner in which a wise parent brings up his child. An outpouring of too much love would only spoil the child; for the child's benefit it is often necessary for the parent to show a severe attitude, and even punish him occasionally. But, clearly, even such punishment is an act of love, except that to the child it appears that the parent does not love him at the moment of the disciplinary action — which is just as well, for otherwise it would make a sham of the discipline.

We can also see that a parent's obvious kindness and benevolence to the child call forth a feeling of love in the child for the parent, while the restraints and disciplines that a parent imposes on the child bring out in him a feeling of fear, awe and respect.

In the same way, G-d's act of *chesed* and *gevurah* call forth in us the feelings of love of G-d and fear of G-d, respectively, both of which are prerequisite to the service of G-d with *all* our heart.

Now, in addition to G-d's Name being "great and awesome," G-d is also *holy.* The term *kadosh,* "holy," implies aloofness and separateness. Thus, while G-d's presence in the world can be seen through His acts of loving-kindness as well as those inspiring awe and fear, G-d Himself is "separate" from the world; He is not affected or changed in any way by what goes on in the world or, indeed, by the creation of the world itself. This attribute of G-d is above and beyond human understanding, since no created being can understand G-d's way, any more than one can understand G-d Himself. This explains also why the "second person" is suddenly changed to the "third" in reference to "holy" ("They will praise *Your* Name... holy is *He*"). The third person (in Hebrew, *nistar*) implies that the person can not be addressed directly, as he is out of sight, "hidden."

"The might of the King is loving justice." When G-d manifests Himself through His tremendous works, especially when He dispenses justice, then people come to know that He is "great, awesome and holy." This will become clear to all on the Day of Reckoning, of which the psalmist speaks here as well as in the preceding psalms. Then all the nations of the world will recognize also the eternal truths of the Torah and Mitzvot, which G-d gave to the Jewish people ("Jacob"), and which the Jewish people has preserved in good times as well as bad throughout the generations. It is the G-d-given Torah and Mitzvot that have made the Jewish nation the bearer of "equity, justice and righteousness" in a world sadly lacking in these Divine qualities.

The psalm continues with a call to exalt G-d, our G-d, repeating "holy is He."

Speaking of G-d's holiness, and of the laws of justice and morality which He has established in His people Israel, the psalmist recalls Mosheh, Aaron and Shmuel (the prophet Samuel) to indicate that it was thanks to such leaders that the Jewish people were able to maintain their high standards of morality and justice. At the same time, the psalmist pointedly reminds us that the leaders themselves were never above the Law. To the contrary, the slightest infringement on the part of a leader is all the more serious by reason of his high position and influence. Our Sages declared that G-d judges the righteous more strictly than ordinary people.[17]

The last verse of Psalm 98 is similar to the fifth, with a call to exalt G-d and bow down to "His footstool" (verse 5), which is the same as "His holy mountain" (in the last verse), namely the *Bet Hamikdash*, "for holy is G-d, our G-d."

---

17. *Yebamot* 121b.

מזמור לדוד
Psalm 29: Mizmor L'David

A Psalm by David:
Give unto the L-rd, O ye children of the mighty,
Give unto the L-rd glory and strength;
Give unto the L-rd glory due unto His Name
Worship the L-rd in the beauty of holiness...

This psalm is of special interest in that it repeats "Give unto the L-rd" three times; it contains G-d's Name eighteen times; it mentions the "voice of G-d" (*kol haShem*) seven times.

The Talmud sees in the threefold repetition of "Give unto the L-rd" an allusion to the first three blessings of the *Amidah,* known as *avot* (patriarchs), *gevurot* (mighty deeds) and *kedushot* (holiness). *Avot* is implied in the first "Give," where "children of the *mighty*" refers to us, children of the patriarchs Abraham, Isaac and Jacob, who are characterized as *elim* ("mighty," or "G-d-like"). The second blessing, *gevurot,* is contained in "Give... *glory and strength.*" The third, *kedushot,* in "Give... *beauty and holiness.*"[18]

Elsewhere in the Talmud[19] Rabbi Hillel, the son of R. Shmuel bar Nachmani, explained that the eighteen benedictions of the *Amidah* correspond to the eighteen times G-d's Name is mentioned in this psalm.[19]

The seven repetitions of the words *kol haShem* ("G-d's voice"), we are told, correspond to the seven days of Creation, when everything was created by G-d's word. They also correspond to the seven Divine attributes by which G-d has created the world and rules it. Thus, "the voice of G-d is upon the waters" refers to the Divine attribute of mercy (*chesed*), symbolized by flowing water; "the voice of G-d is powerful" refers to the attribute of *gevurah,* and so forth.

---

18. *Rosh Hashanah* 32a; *Megillah* 17a.
19. *Berachot* 28b.

Our Sages also see in the seven repetitions of *kol* ("voice") a symbolic reminder of the Giving of the Torah at Sinai, when the words *kol* or *kolot* are again mentioned seven times.

In the writings of the saintly Ari (Rabbi Yitzchak Luria), the special significance of this psalm is discussed in detail, declaring that a far-reaching and tremendous effect takes place in the Upper Worlds when this psalm is recited with *kavanah* (concentration) and joy. We also learn of the significance of the *eleven* verses of this psalm and its *ninety-one* letters.

But one need not be versed in Lurianic Kabbalah for this psalm to arouse much joy and inspiration; one need only reflect on even one of the thoughts that King David expresses in this psalm written for every Jew — that we are the children of our forefathers, Abraham, Isaac and Jacob, and have been given the privilege of appreciating G-d's loving-kindness, might and holiness, and of sharing in these Divine qualities.

There is another reason why this psalm should be recited with great joy. Psalm 29 was the Song of the Day (*Shir-shel-Yom*) for the first day of *Chol Hamoed Succot*.[20] The reason for the choice of this psalm, as *Rashi* explains, it was the day of the great Celebration of the Water-Drawing (*Simchat Bet Hashoevah*) for the water offering on the Altar, to which the words "G-d's voice is up on the waters" allude.

Perhaps the most significant verse of the psalm is the one with which it concludes:

The L-rd will give strength to His people;
The L-rd will bless His people with peace.

Our Sages of the Talmud[21] declare that by "strength" (*oz*) King David alludes to the Mitzvah of *tefillin*, for it is in reference to *tefillin* that the Torah says: "And all the nations of the world will see that the Name of G-d is called upon you, and they will

---

20. *Succah* 55a.
21. *Berachot* 6a.

fear you."[22] This is to say that the Mitzvah of *tefillin* has a special quality of giving the Jewish people divine power, inspiring awe and fear in the hearts of their enemies so that they would not dare harm them. Thus G-d will bless His people with peace.

Oz, our Sages also say, refers to the Torah itself. indeed, the *Targum* translates this verse "G-d gives the Torah to the Jewish people." In giving us the Torah, G-d has given us the possibility to attach ourselves to Him through the study and the observance of the Mitzvot — the source of our real strength.

It is noteworthy that the *Mishnayot* (the *Torah-shebe'al Peh*) concludes with the quotation of the final verse of this psalm. Rabbi Shimon ben Halafta said, the Holy One blessed be He, found no vessel that could contain blessings for the Jewish people except peace, for so it is written, "G-d will give strength to His people, G-d will bless His people with peace." Peace (*Shalom*) is the "vessel" that contains all blessings.[23]

לכה דודי
Lecha Dodi

We are all familiar with this beautiful and inspiring hymn of the Friday night service (*Kabbalat Shabbat*). It was composed by the saintly Kabbalist, Rabbi Shlomo Halevi Alkabetz, who died in Safed, in the Holy Land, in about the year 1580. He was one of the leading Kabbalists in Safed, a contemporary of Rabbi Moshe Cordovero (his brother-in-law and disciple), Rabbi Moshe Alshich and Rabbi Yitzchak Luria, founder of the Lurianic Kabbalah. It was due to the great authority of the last-named that the hymn *Lecha Dodi* was adopted and included in

---

22. Deuteronomy 28:10.
23. End of *Oktzin.*

Kabbalat Shabbat in both Ashkenazi and Sephardi communities all over the world.

The author "signed" his name in the initial letters of the eight stanzas of the hymn, beginning with the letter "shin" (*"Shamor v'zachor,"* etc.), which spell out his name, Shlomo Halevi. For this reason, incidentally, the saintly poet reversed the order, putting *shamor* before *zachor.* For inasmuch as these two words refer to the first words of the Fifth Commandment as it appears in the two versions of the Ten Commandments (in Exodus — *zachor* — "Remember the Shabbat day to keep it holy," and later in Deuteronomy — *shamor* — "Keep the Shabbat day holy"), it would have been more correct to say *"Zachor v'shamor."* Actually, since both words were spoken simultaneously,[24] as the poet opens his hymn, *"Keep* and *Remember* in a *single* utterance...",* the meaning of the phrase is not changed by the transposition.

The refrain of this hymn, *"Lecha Dodi"* and, indeed, the entire motif of the hymn, in which the Shabbat is represented as a "Queen" whom we go out to welcome, is based on a Talmudic source,[25] where we are told how two great Sages welcomed the Shabbat. Rabbi Chanina used to dress himself in honor of Shabbat and say (to his disciples): "Come, let us go out to welcome the Shabbat Queen." Rabbi Yannai, dressed in his Shabbat clothes, would announce: *"Bo'i Kallah, bo'i Kallah* — Come in, Bride; come in, Bride."[25]

An earlier source, quotes Rabbi Shimon ben Yochai (author of the *Zohar*) as follows:

When G-d created the world in six days and rested on the seventh day, which He blessed and made holy, Shabbat appeared before the Holy One, blessed be He, and complained: "Master of the universe, each day of the week has a mate, but I

---

24. *Mechilta* on Exodus 20:8.
25. *Shabbat* 119a.

am the odd one, without a mate!"[26] Replied G-d: "The Jewish people will be your mate." Thus, when G-d gave His Torah to the Jewish people at Sinai, He began the Fifth Commandment with the words, "Remember the Shabbat day to keep it holy," as if to say, "Remember the promise I made to the Shabbat that the Jewish people will be its mate."[27]

It should be noted that the word *l'kadsho*, "to keep it holy," also means "to betroth it" — an allusion to the special relationship between the Jewish people and the Shabbat as that of "bride" and "groom."

Thus, the great Sage and father of the Kabbalists, Rabbi Shimon ben Yochai, tells us in his quaint way that from the beginning of the Creation of the world, the Shabbat and the Jewish people were destined for each other and bound together with bonds of devotion, loyalty and joy.

This theme of bride and groom — symbolic also of the mutual affection and devotion between the Jewish people and G-d, as well as between the Jewish people and the Torah, permeates the Song of Songs (*Shir haShirim*) composed by King Solomon. Indeed, it is from this holy book (one of the five *Megillot* of *T'NaCh*) that the name of the hymn and its refrain — *"Lecha Dodi"* — is derived.[28] This is also the reason why in some communities it is customary to recite *Shir HaShirim* on Friday afternoon, before ushering in the Shabbat bride.

---

26. The seven days of the week may be divided into three pairs of days, each pair adding up to seven (one and six; two and five; three and four), leaving the seventh day as a single day.
27. See also *Bereishit Rabbah* 11:9.
28. Song of Songs 7:12.

שמור וזכור
Shamor V'Zachor

"Keep" and "remember" in a single utterance
The One G-d caused us to hear
G-d is One and His name is One
For renown, glory and praise."

Our Sages[29] explain that the two versions of the Fourth Commandment: "Remember the Shabbat day to keep it holy..."[30] and "Keep the Shabbat day holy..."[31] were pronounced simultaneously by G-d at Mount Sinai, yet both were clearly heard by all the people. This was a double miracle, since no human being can utter two different syllables at the same time, nor can one make sense of any two words coming simultaneously from two persons. But then the entire Divine Revelation at Sinai, when the whole Jewish people heard the voice of G-d coming through the flame and cloud enveloping the mountain, was a series of wonderful miracles, never before and never since experienced in the history of mankind.

The fact that the Shabbat commandment was given in such a miraculous way emphasizes the very nature of Shabbat itself, which is supernatural and miraculous. This is also brought out in the next stanza, which will be discussed later.

Referring to the two expressions, "remember" (*zachor*) and "keep" (*shamor*), our Sages explain that the first, *zachor*, refers to and includes all the positive precepts (*Mitzvot-asseh*), the "do's" connected with Shabbat observance, such as *kiddush*, prayer, Torah-study, as well as such "material" things as changing into Shabbat clothes, having special Shabbat meals — in

29. *Mechilta* on Exodus 20:8.
30. Exodus 20:8.
31. Deuteronomy 5:12.

short, all the things we *do* for the honor and holiness of the Shabbat day.

"Keep," *shamor,* (literally "beware of") refers to all the "do not's" connected with Shabbat observance, namely, *not to do* any of the thirty-nine kinds of actions defined as "work," with all their offshoots. These have nothing to do with the actual effort involved, for it is a desecration of Shabbat to turn on the electric light as it is to plow the field.

Furthermore, noting that *zachor* and *shamor* were pronounced in a single utterance, our Sages of the Talmud explain that it was not to demonstrate that G-d can perform miracles. It was to indicate that both kinds of Mitzvot, the "do's" and the "do not's," relating to Shabbat, apply equally to both men and women. For usually only the prohibitions (*lo ta'aseh*) of the Torah apply to both men and women, while many of the positive precepts involving a time-element (such as *tzitzit,* which are limited to daytime; *succah* and many others) are not binding on women. Accordingly, at first glance one might have thought that the "do's" of Shabbat would not apply to women. Therefore, by pronouncing *zachor* and *shamor* in one utterance, G-d made it clear that the "do's" and the "do not's" of Shabbat apply equally to men and women.

There is one great and beautiful Mitzvah which has been made the privilege of the woman, namely, the lighting of the candles (at least 18 minutes before sunset on the eve of Shabbat). It is customary for the wife to light at least two candles, one for *zachor* and one for *shamor.* Our Sages speak with extraordinary reverence and in mystical terms of this great Mitzvah and special privilege of the Jewish woman. They point out that by lighting the Shabbat candles Jewish women help spread the "tabernacle of peace" (*succat-shalom*) over our people, and illuminate the souls that are the "lights" of the world. Moreover, in the merit of this great Mitzvah, the wife is blessed with fine children, shining with the light of Torah. She also brings the blessing of long life to her husband. No other Mitzvah by man or woman is more rewarding than that of lighting the Shabbat candles by the wife and mother, in recognition of her being the *akeret habayit*, the foundation of the Jewish home and of the House of Jacob.[32]

The Lubavitcher Rebbe, Rabbi Menachem M. Schneerson, שליט״א, has strongly urged that unmarried women and little girls old enough to be trained in Jewish customs and Mitzvot, from about the age of three years and older, should also light their own candle before Shabbat and recite the blessing over it. He has declared that this is especially vital now that the peace of the world in general, and of our people in particular, is so gravely threatened. "In a world plunged in darkness," he has said, "each and every Jewish girl lighting a Shabbat candle helps bring a little more pure light into the home and into the world, and all G-d's blessings that go with it."

*　　*　　*

The words "G-d is One and His name is One" seem repetitious, having already referred to the "only G-d." However, having said that *shamor* and *zachor* came from G-d in a single utterance, the poet seems to allude to the mystery of this particular miracle. G-d is one perfect Unity, and just as He is capable of creating the whole world, with so many different things, without it affecting His Unity, so He is, of course, capable of uttering two or more words simultaneously. A human being, like all other things G-d has created, is necessarily limited in all his faculties, senses and capacities. But G-d is unlimited in His actions. We have already had occasion to discuss the meaning of G-d's Name.[33] Let us just say briefly here: G-d is One, but He has many names, each one indicative of a particular Divine attribute or action, as it is revealed to us, His creatures. But *all* His names are really *one,* since His attributes and actions do not affect His perfect unity in the slightest. This, too, is something no human

---

32. *Zohar, Bereishit* 48b. See also pp. 78-79 below.
33. See p. 19 ff.

being can fathom because human intellectual capacity is
limited.[34]

The words, "for renown, glory and praise," are taken (and
rearranged for the purpose of the rhyme) from the verse: "to
observe all (G-d's) commandments...for praise, renown and
glory."[35] All G-d's commandments, and especially the Shabbat,
are the eternal values that distinguish the Jewish people from the
nations of the world. It is in these sacred laws of the Torah,
which we observe in our daily life, that we rightfully take pride,
and it is in these Divine laws, which make for a holy and truly
worthy life, that the "chosenness" of our people is expressed.

לקראת שבת
Likrat Shabbat

Come, let us go to welcome the Shabbat
For it is the source of blessing;
From the beginning, from of old, it was crowned
Last in creation, first in thought.

In the second stanza of *Lecha Dodi*, the poet calls us to join
him in welcoming the Shabbat. In olden days it was actually the
custom to welcome the Shabbat under the open sky.

The poet reminds us that the Shabbat is the source of blessings. The *Zohar* quotes the sage, Rabbi Yitzchak, who, referring
to the verse "And G-d blessed the seventh day,"[35a] declares that
"all the blessings of the upper and lower worlds derive from the
seventh day," and that "all the six days of the week are blessed

---

34. In Chabad the subject of G-d's Unity is discussed at great length
    and made somewhat more comprehensible. See Nissan Mindel,
    The Philosophy of Chabad, Kehot Publication Society, 3rd ed.,
    1985.
35. Deuteronomy 26:19.
35a. Genesis 2:3.

through this seventh day, Shabbat."[35b] Many other sages quoted in the Zohar and in the Talmud speak of Shabbat as the source and wellspring of all G-d's blessings, both spiritual and material. Rabbi Yehuda sums it up: "He who delights in the Shabbat sees all his heart's desires fulfilled."[36]

Throughout the ages, no matter how difficult it was to keep the Shabbat, Jews considered it no sacrifice to close their businesses and abstain from work on this holy day. Knowing that Shabbat was the source of all blessings for the six days of the week, they realized that it would be foolish to desecrate it. For not only would money gained so wrongfully be of no lasting value, it would also deprive the other six days of G-d's blessings. So the sensible Jew always tries to train for the kind of job or open the kind of business and live in the kind of environment where he can fully observe Shabbat and *Yom Tov*. He wants to earn money not for its own sake, but for the good purposes to which he can put it; not, G-d forbid, for doctor's bills and the like. In this way he assures himself that Rabbi Yehuda's promise will be fulfilled for him and his family.

The poet goes on to say that the special nature of Shabbat — its being blessed and bestowing blessing, and its being holy and bestowing holiness — was ordained by G-d from the beginning of creation, when the Shabbat was "anointed" (*nesuchah*) as "Queen." And although Shabbat came *last in creation*, for it was proclaimed by G-d as the holy day of rest after all things had been created during the preceding six days, it was, however, *first in the Divine thought*. The *Midrash* explains it by the following illustration: "A king prepared a beautiful canopy, and decorated it lavishly. What remained to complete it? The bride, of course." Clearly, while the king was making the canopy and decorating it, he had in mind the bride he had chosen. And so it was with the

---

35[b]. *Zohar, Beshallach* 63b; *Yitro* 88b.
36. *Shabbat* 118a.

King of the Universe, who created the whole world for the Shabbat Queen.[37]

Thus, the Jew works and toils during the six days of the week
in order to prepare for Shabbat and be able to enjoy it and
delight in it. From the first day of the week he already looks
forward to it, and counts the days to Shabbat. This is why we say
before reciting the daily psalm (*Shir-shel-Yom*): "Today is the
first day in Shabbat" (*Hayom yom rishon baShabbat*) or "Today
is the second day in Shabbat," and so on. We do not say *basha-
vua* ("in the week"). In this way we not only remember the
Shabbat every day of the week and look forward to it, but we
also realize that the whole week is called "Shabbat" in the sense
that Shabbat gives meaning and content to each day of the week,
is its source of blessing, and, indeed, its very soul; or, as the poet
expresses it, "first in thought."

מקדש מלך

Mikdash Melech

Sanctuary of (our) King, Regal City,
Arise, come out of the upheaval!
Long enough have you dwelt in the valley of weeping,
And He will have compassion for you.

In this stanza, as in all the following, the poet addresses himself to the Holy City, Jerusalem, which personifies the Jewish
people. He speaks of the restoration and glory of Jerusalem
which will come with the final redemption of our people through
our righteous *Mashiach*, as G-d had promised through His holy
prophets.

The "Sanctuary of the King" (Mikdash Melech) — Jerusalem
— is a title borrowed from the prophet Amos. It is also called
"regal city" for the same reason, namely, because in it the pres-

---

37. *Bereishit Rabbah* 10:9.

ence of G-d, our Supreme King, was particularly felt, especially
in the *Bet Hamikdash,* the very "heart" of the Holy City. Jerusalem was also the royal residence of the House of David, and will
again be the residence of the *Melech haMashiach.*

The "upheaval" refers to the *galut* (exile), also called "valley
of weeping."[38] Many tears have we shed in the lands of our
dispersion, in exile among hostile nations; tears not only of
suffering, but also of longing for our homeland and for our
reunion with the Divine *Shechinah* in the "Sanctuary of our
King."

Emek habacha ("valley of weeping") also means "valley of
confusion (or perplexity)," according to *Rashi* on Isaiah 9:17,
being derived from the same root as *nevuchim* ("perplexed") in
Exodus 14:3. Maimonides called his famous philosophical work
"*Moreh Nevuchim*" (Guide for the Perplexed).

Both meanings, "weeping" and "confusion," accurately describe our *galut.*

To understand more deeply the expressions used by our poet-
Kabbalist, Rabbi Shlomo Alkabetz, in this stanza, we have to
refer to the Kabbalah concept of our world as three-dimensional. They call the three dimensions *olam, shanah, nefesh,* which,
freely translated, mean "space," "time" and "life." In each of
them, G-d set apart an especially holy and unique element: in
time — the Shabbat; in space — the Holy Land, especially Jerusalem; and in life — the Jewish people (by virtue of the Torah
and Mitzvot).

Briefly:[39] The term "royalty" in the Kabbalah is generally
understood also in the sense of "influence," just as a king rules
by his influence, which extends from his royal person to each
and every subject in his kingdom.

It is in this sense that Shabbat is called "Queen," because its
influence extends to each and every day of the week.

---

38. Psalms 84:7.
39. The discussion that follows by no means exhausts the subject.

Similarly, Jerusalem is called "Regal City" — because its influence is felt in every corner of the world, and the Jewish people is called a "kingdom of priests" — because of its spiritual influence on all humanity.

Each of the three — Shabbat, Jerusalem, the people of Israel — derives its royalty and holiness from the King of Kings, the Holy One, blessed be He, our G-d and Creator, by reason of G-d's choice and appointment. It is just as a king chooses and appoints his ministers because of their special fitness for the particular service, and then bestows upon them special honor and power to rule in the king's name and by his authority.

In order of appearance, Shabbat came first, for it was the seventh day of creation that G-d made into a holy day of rest.

The holiness and royalty of the Jewish people was established when the Jewish people received the Torah and Mitzvot at Mount Sinai, seven weeks after their liberation from Egyptian bondage.

The Holy Land came forty years later, when the Jewish people took possession of the Promised Land, previously called the land of Canaan. Jerusalem became the Holy City when G-d chose it as the site of the *Bet Hamikdash.*

Thus the three chosen ones — Shabbat, Jerusalem and the Jewish people — became inseparably linked together. Shabbat without the Jewish people is as unthinkable as the Jewish people without Shabbat, and Jerusalem is as empty without Jews as the Jewish people would be empty without all that Jerusalem stands for.

However, in the present era of the *galut,* where darkness and confusion reign supreme, this unity is sometimes blurred, or even disrupted. This is why the poet calls the *galut* "upheaval" (*mahapechah*), a word first used in the Torah in connection with the upheaval of Sodom[40] when Sodom and its three sister cities were turned upside down. Such is the upheaval of the *galut* that,

_____

40. Genesis 19:29.

instead of honoring the Jewish people and feeling deeply grateful for all it has done for mankind through the ages, the nations of the world hate, despise and persecute the Jewish people, with not infrequent outbursts of horrible cruelty and inhumanity, and the worst enemy of the Jews can become the greatest hero and leader among the nations.

Moreover, such is the darkness and confusion of the *galut* that Jews, too, sometimes find themselves quite perplexed, and act in a contrary manner. Some Jews try to copy non-Jews in every way: they do not realize that by neglecting the Jewish way of life, the way of Torah and Mitzvot, they turn their life upside down. Even some who have faith in G-d, can yet do things that are contrary to G-d's Will, like the thief who hopes to make a successful burglary "with the help of G-d."[41]

In all this confusion and darkness of the *galut*, a Jew has only to turn to the Torah and Mitzvot to light up his path, as it is written, "A Mitzvah is a lamp, and the Torah is light."[42] Shabbat is particularly effective in dispelling the darkness and confusion of the *galut*, as this is symbolized also by the lighting of the Shabbat candles. This meaningful and great Mitzvah, which is the personal privilege of the Jewish mother and daughter, truly lights up the Jewish home and life. But Shabbat observance goes even further than that. Not only does it help sweep away the darkness of the *galut*, but also the *Galut* itself. Thus, our Sages declared, "If the entire Jewish people would only observe two Shabbatot properly, they would immediately be redeemed."[43] Then, with the appearance of our Righteous Redeemer, all the Jewish exiles will be gathered into the Holy Land, and the *Bet Hamikdash* will be rebuilt on its former site in Jerusalem. The unity of the three "dimensions" — Shabbat, Jerusalem and the Jewish people — will then be restored and fully realized in actual

---

41. *Berachot* 63a (according to the version of *Eyn Yaakov*).
42. Proverbs 6:29.
43. *Shabbat* 118b.

life. This will bring about the perfect world, what our Sages call
"a world which is all Shabbat"[44] — the ultimate fulfillment of
Creation.

התנערי

Hitna'ari

Shake off the dust, arise!
Put on your clothes of glory, O my people
Through the son of Yishai of Bet Lechem,
Come close to my soul, redeem it.

Addressing himself to Jerusalem as a symbol of the Jewish
people, the poet calls upon it to, in the words of our prophet
Isaiah,[45] "Shake off the dust and get up," as one would to a
person who has fallen or has been humbled to the dust. It is a
figure of speech indicating a complete recovery from a humiliating situation — in this case, the destruction of Jerusalem and the
humiliating exile of the Jewish people.

In a deeper sense, the poet may be speaking not only of the
physical restoration of Jerusalem, but also of the spiritual recovery of the Jewish people. For, when the Jews were dispersed in
exile among heathen and otherwise morally backward peoples, it
was inevitable that some Jews would pick up un-Jewish traits
and habits. This is the "dust" of the *galut* that clings to some
Jews, trying slavishly to imitate their non-Jewish neighbors.
Sometimes this layer of dust is so heavy that one can hardly
recognize the Jew beneath it. Yet, it is only a superficial layer,
which can only hide, but not extinguish, the Jewish spark that
always remains alive in a Jew. All that is therefore necessary is to
shake off this "dust," and the real person, the real Jew, emerges

---

44. *Mishnah* end of *Tamid*.
45. Isaiah 52:2.

and reveals himself in all his glory. This is also the meaning of
the poet's call, again in the words of Isaiah: "Put on your clothes
of glory, O my people." In other words, *be my people*, be your
old self again!

What are the Jew's "clothes of glory"? These are the Mitzvot
which the Jew performs in his everyday life. As has been mentioned before, the study of the Torah nourishes the soul, while
the performance of its Mitzvot "clothes" the soul. Commitment
to the Torah and Mitzvot is a necessary preparation for the
coming of *Mashiach*, who will be a descendant of David the son
of Yishai of Bet Lechem. This prompts the poet to utter a short
prayer to G-d: "Come close to my soul, redeem it." Thus, the
geula (redemption) that *Mashiach* will bring will be complete,
both for the Jewish people as a whole, and for each and every
Jew individually.

התעוררי

Hit'oreri

Arouse yourself, arouse yourself,
For your light is come; arise, shine forth!
Awake, awake, give forth a song,
The glory of G-d is revealed upon you.

This rousing call to an awakening and an exciting welcome of
the *geula*, which the poet expresses here so vividly, has the familiar ring of Isaiah's *geula* prophecies.[46]

Echoing the words of the prophet, the poet calls upon the
Jewish people to wake up from its sleep, the *galut*. The use of
"sleep" as a metaphor for the exile is meaningful in many ways.
Sleep is a state of suspended animation. While a person sleeps,
he is unconscious of what is happening around him. His mind is

---

46. Isaiah 51:17, 52:1, 60:1, etc.

asleep, as is his ability to understand and reason. With his rational faculties at rest, imagination takes over, giving rise to dreams and fancies.

We have already discussed the subject of the *galut* as it is described in terms of dreams[46a] and nightmares. The things that happen to Jews in *galut* among the nations of the world are often so strange and irrational as to be unbelievable. The hatred, the persecutions, the massacres, the holocaust — these are things that one would think could happen only in nightmares. Unfortunately, they did happen. This is why the *galut* is one long nightmare.

But, one will ask, if there are such beastly nations and individuals who are capable of such atrocities towards a defenseless minority in their midst, why did not G-d protect the Jews? The answer is that G-d's protection of the Jewish people is inseparable from the Jews' adherence to the Torah and Mitzvot. The Torah and Mitzvot are the Divine protective shield for Jews against their enemies. When Jewish adherence to Torah and Mitzvot weakens, this shield weakens and wears thin. This happens when, under the influence of the long *galut*-night, some Jews become drowsy, or "fall asleep," in matters of Torah and Mitzvot.

And so the poet calls upon the Jewish people to wake up from its sleep, since the night of the *galut* is about over, and the dawn of the *geula* is about to break through the gloom. It is time to wake up and sing the song of the *geula* just as Mosheh *Rabbeinu* and the children of Israel sang the song of salvation after their liberation from the Egyptian *galut*.

The entire stanza is a paraphrase of Isaiah's prophecies, particularly the verse, "Arise, shine forth, for your light is come, and the glory of G-d has shone upon you."[47]

46a. Nissan Mindel, *My Prayer* pub. by Merkos L'inyonei Chinuch,
     6th ed. 1984, Vol. I, pp. 284-286.
47. Isaiah 60:1.

לא תבושי
Lo Teivoshi

You shall not be ashamed, nor disgraced.
Why are you cast down, and why are you disquieted?
In you the poor of my people shall trust,
And the City shall be rebuilt on its mound.

Continuing the theme of the final redemption, the poet assures the Jewish people that they shall never be ashamed or disgraced again. This, too, is a paraphrase of the words of the prophet Isaiah[48]: "Fear not, for you shall not be ashamed," etc. The nature of this fear is that in past redemptions — from Egypt and from the Babylonian exile — painful reverses were later suffered by our people. The redemptions were not everlasting for, after the *geula* from Egypt, there was the exile into Babylon, and after the return from Babylon, Jerusalem was destroyed a second time, and there was exile and dispersion, the long and bitter *galut* which is still upon us. But after the next *geula,* being the final and complete redemption, the poet assures us, there will never again be any disappointments, or any fear of being put to shame and disgrace again. There is no reason, therefore, to be "cast down" and "disquieted" — a phrase borrowed from Psalms.[49]

Addressing himself to Jerusalem, the poet assures the Holy City that it will again be a safe and trustworthy haven for Jews returning to it from all parts of the world. This line (the third of the stanza) is also taken from Isaiah, which reads, "G-d has founded Zion, and *the poor of His people* shall trust (i.e., find safe haven) in it."[50] According to *Rashi,* "the poor of His people" include also the ten tribes (who had been exiled by Shalma-

---

48. Isaiah 54:4.
49. Psalms 42:12.
50. Isaiah 14:32.

neser of Assyria some 133 years before the destruction of
Jerusalem by Nebuchadnezar of Babylon).

The last line of the stanza is taken from Yirmiyahu: "Thus says
G-d: Behold, I will bring back the captivity of Jacob's tents and
have mercy upon his dwelling places, and *the City shall be rebuilt
on its mound* (i.e., on its former site), and the Palace (i.e., the *Bet
Hamikdash*) shall be restored as of old."[51]

והיו למשסה

Vehayu Limshisa

*And they that spoil you shall be a spoil
All your destroyers shall be far away;
Your G-d shall rejoice over you
As a bridegroom rejoices over his bride.*

This stanza, too, like the others, is constructed of quotations
from the prophets Isaiah and Yirmiyahu.

Yirmiyahu declares: *"They that spoil* (plunder) *you shall be a
spoil, and all that plunder you I will put to plunder."*[52]

Isaiah, addressing himself to Zion (Jerusalem), declares:
"Your ruins and your desolate places, and your destroyed land,
shall now become crowded with inhabitants, *and all your destroyers shall be far away."*[53]

Jerusalem had been destroyed and plundered many times, and
the Holy Land had been laid waste. But G-d assured us, through
His holy prophets, that not only will Jerusalem be rebuilt on its
former site, but that all the waste and desolate cities and villages
of our land will be rebuilt and, indeed, will become more
crowded than ever before by Jews returning to their homeland
from all corners of the earth.

---

51. Jeremiah 30:18.
52. Jeremiah 30:16.
53. Isaiah 49:19.

The next two lines are taken from Isaiah, where the prophet describes the joy of the Jews' return to their land, and of the new attachment between G-d and His people as the joy of a bride and bridegroom.[54] The famed commentator Rabbi David Kimchi (*RaDaK*) makes a penetrating observation of this analogy. He says that just as a bridegroom and bride are most faithful to each other, to the exclusion of anyone else, so the land of Israel, when it was laid waste by other nations, never accepted other inhabitants, and remained waste and desolate for many centuries. Only the Jewish people, its true children, are welcomed by it, and to Jews alone does the land readily respond, rejoicing with them like a bride and bridegroom that belong to each other.

ימין ושמאל

Yamin Usmol

You shall spread forth to the right and to the left
And you shall revere G-d;
Through an offspring of Peretz
We shall rejoice and be glad.

Like the previous stanzas, this too consists of fragments from the *geula* prophecies of Isaiah. The first line is taken from Isaiah which reads: "For you shall spread forth to the right hand and to the left, and your seed shall inherit nations, and shall inhabit (hitherto) desolate cities."[55] The poet assures us in the words of the prophet that when the time of the *Geula* comes, the Jewish people will break through the constraints and blockades set up by our enemies on the right and on the left, and so great will be the miraculous victory that it will call forth a spirit of reverence for G-d.

---

54. Isaiah 62:5.
55. Isaiah 54:3.

The redeemer — *Mashiach* — is here referred to as "an off-spring of Peretz." Peretz and Zerach were twin sons of Yehuda, Jacob's leading son, whom Jacob blessed to be like a lion, the symbol of royalty. The Torah tells us that Peretz "broke through" (this is why he was called Peretz") and was born first.[56] The poet gives us here a beautiful play on words — *tifrotzi* ("you shall spread forth," literally "break through") and *ben Partzi* ("offspring of Peretz"). King David, the son of Yishai, was a descendant of Peretz, as the line of descent is given at the end of the Book of Ruth, and Mashiach will be a descendant of the Royal House of David. The expression *ben Partzi* in reference to *Mashiach* is already found in the *Midrash*.[57]

"We shall rejoice and be glad" is also a part of a well-known verse: "And it shall be said on that day, behold, this is our G-d; we have waited for Him and He will save us; this is our L-rd for whom we have waited, *we will be glad and rejoice* in His salvation."[58]

בואי בשלום

Bo'ie Beshalom

Come in peace; crown of her Husband,
Also with joyous song and with cheerfulness;
In the midst of the faithful of the treasured people
Come in, O Bride, come in, O Bride,
Come in, O Bride, Shabbat Queen.

This is the final stanza of the beautiful poem *Lecha Dodi*. For the recitation of these lines, the congregation and the reader rise and turn around to face the west entrance of the synagogue, as if

---

56. Genesis 38:29.
57. *Bereishit Rabbah* 12:5.
58. Isaiah 25:9.

actually extending a welcome to the Shabbat bride, saying, "Come in, come in, come in — thrice welcome!"

The word *b'shalom* ("in peace") can also, and perhaps even better, be rendered *"with* peace," and this would be more in keeping with the words in the second line ("also with joyous song," etc.). Shabbat brings peace, our Sages say — peace in the upper worlds as well as peace in this (lowest) world of ours. It brings a holy, blissful peace, as well as peace of mind, such as cannot be felt in the mundane days of the week. This is why the Shabbat is also referred to as the "tabernacle of peace" (*Succat-shalom*).

A good Jewish wife is also called in Scripture the "crown of her husband," as it is written, "A woman of worth (*eishet chayil*) is the crown of her husband." But so great is the devotion and love of the Jewish people for the Shabbat that we continue to call her endearingly "Bride," as if we had just "married" her.

According to a further interpretation (in the *Zohar* and Kabbalah), this "welcome" is estended also to the *Shechinah*, the Divine Presence, which accompanies the Shabbat, for the *Shechinah* and the Jewish people are also called bride and groom. This is a particularly meaningful thought, since with the coming of Shabbat every Jew receives a *neshamah yeteirah*, an "extra soul," an extra measure of G-dliness and holiness. The special Shabbat soul dwells in us for the duration of the Shabbat, and departs at *Havdalah*, with the departure of the Shabbat. It enables us to absorb the extra measure of holiness that comes to each of us with the holy Shabbat.[59]

Thus, both the Shabbat and the *Shechinah* are welcomed into "the midst of the treasured people (*am segulah*)." This is the designation that G-d gave our Jewish people when we accepted the Torah.[60] Mosheh *Rabbeinu* reminded the people again when

59. *Zohar II, Yitro* 88b; *II, Pinchas* 242b; *Ha'azinu* 288b; *Tikkunei Zohar* 61.
60. Exodus 19:5.

he took leave of them: "For you are a holy nation unto G-d your G-d; it is you that G-d your G-d chose to be unto Him a treasured people (*am segulah*) from among all the nations on the face of the earth."[61] Here the Torah clearly states the nature of our "chosenness" — not for power, not for riches, not for dominion over other nations, but to be a holy nation, to lead a holy life in the service of G-d in every detail of our daily life.

It is customary when saying, "Come in, O Bride!" to bow to the left and again to the right, as if bowing in reverence to a royal person. The third time, "Come in, O Bride, Shabbat Queen," is said in a whisper (according to the *Ari* custom), while turning to the front of the synagogue again. On this note, the beautiful hymn *Lecha Dodi* concludes.

מזמור שיר ליום השבת
Psalm 92: Mizmor Shir L'Yom HaShabbat

The *Shir-shel-Yom* (Song of the Day) that the Levites used to chant in the *Bet Hamikdash* on the day of Shabbat was Psalm 92 of *Tehillim, Mizmor Shir l'Yom haShabbat.*

On the seventh day of Creation, all "work" of creation had ceased, and G-d "rested" and made this day a holy day, a day of rest. Here, "work" and "rest," insofar as G-d is concerned, are not to be understood in the plain sense of the words, as they are used in regard to human beings. For when a human being does any kind of work or activity, he uses up some of his energy, and at the end of the day gets tired and has to rest. But it was no effort at all for G-d to create the world, as it is written, "By the *word* of G-d the heavens were made, and by the *breath of His mouth* — all their hosts."[62] Everything was created by G-d's "word," and the whole of creation did not make any change in

---

61. Deuteronomy 7:6.
62. Psalms 33:6.

G-d, just as, by way of example, a spoken word does not cause a change in a human being. On the seventh day, G-d did not create anything new, except the Shabbat itself as a day of rest and holiness.

The Jewish people have been commanded to "imitate" G-d in all His ways. So we were commanded to work during the six days of the week and to rest on the seventh day and keep it holy. Since we consist of a body and a soul, the commandment to work and to rest applies to both the body and the soul. In other words, Shabbat has a two-fold meaning, both physical and spiritual. The first simply means that we are commanded to stop before sunset on Friday, all and any of the 39 kinds of *creative* physical activities and their offshoots, as are clearly spelled out in Jewish law; and to dedicate the seventh day, Shabbat, entirely to G-d, to *holy* pursuits. There is a complete change-over in our routine. Even our physical needs: our food, clothes, our walking and talking, everything is different and special — *Shabbosdik* (Shabbat-like). We use the word "creative" in describing physical work that is prohibited on Shabbat because the important thing here is not the actual physical exertion. It is the creative aspect that is "similar" to G-d's acts of creation during the Six Days of Creation. It is easier to strike a match or turn an electric switch that is a *creative* form of work than moving a heavy chair from place to place inside the house; yet the former is prohibited while the latter is permitted.

The second aspect of Shabbat has to do purely with our *soul*, which also enjoys a "rest" on Shabbat. By this we mean that during the six days of the week the soul has somewhat of a struggle in carrying out its purpose of bringing holiness into our everyday activities. For we Jews are a holy people not only on Shabbat and *Yom Tov*, but every day of the year. Not only do we pray and perform Mitzvot every day, but all our activities, including our eating, drinking and business dealings, have to be done according to G-d's will, as required by Jewish law. This entails spiritual effort. On Shabbat, however, our soul receives

from Heaven a special measure of holiness and inspiration —
the *neshamah yeteirah* ("additional soul") — so that the holiness
comes without effort, and we enjoy a special spiritual joy and
restfulness we call *oneg* Shabbat.

> *Thus, Shabbat is a day when it is good to give thanks*
> *unto G-d, and to sing praises unto Your most high*
> *Name.*[63]

In a broader sense, our life on earth is likened to the "working
days" of the week, while our after-life is likened to Shabbat,
when we truly enjoy the fruits of our labors here on earth, in the
higher spiritual degree of the soul's release from her earthly
chains. Thus gaining immediate nearness to G-d.

Shabbat and the weekdays are, in a sense, like day and night.
Similarly our life in the *galut* is likened to the dark night, while
our redemption when *Mashiach* will come, and the change that
will then be brought about, is likened to the dawn of a new day.
This is expressed in the next verse, "To declare Your loving-
kindness in the morning, and Your faithfulness in the night."[64]
In the "morning" we can see G-d's loving-kindness; in the
"night" we have to have *faith* in G-d's kindness, because it often
comes as a "blessing in disguise."

Shabbat is the day when we can reflect upon G-d's works and
derive extraordinary joy in appreciating them, as we read:

> *For You, O G-d, have made me rejoice with Your work;*
> *in the works of Your hand I will exult. How great are*
> *Your works, O G-d; Your thoughts are very deep.*[65]

The Shabbat gives us a better appreciation of, and deeper
insights into, the whole order of the world that G-d has created.
G-d created man so that he would have free choice to do as he
pleases. It is inevitable that there should be wicked men who
rebel against G-d. But G-d reigns supreme, and He is a G-d of

63. Ps. 92 v. 2.
64. Ibid. v. 3.
65. Ibid. vs. 5-6.

justice. If the wicked appear to prosper, it is only because they are to perish, but the righteous will triumph. This is the thought in the following verses:

> A brutish man will not know, neither will the fool understand this: When the wicked spring up as grass, all doers of iniquity bloom forth — it is that they might be destroyed forever. But You, O G-d, are On High for evermore.... The righteous man shall flourish like a palm-tree; he shall grow like a cedar in Lebanon. Planted in the house of G-d, they shall blossom in the courts of our G-d. They shall still produce fruit in old age; they shall be full of sap and freshness. To declare that G-d is upright; He is my Rock, and there is no unrighteousness in Him.[66]

"The righteous (tzaddik) shall flourish like a date palm, like a cedar in Lebanon," says the psalmist. Our Sages give various reasons why the righteous man has been likened to the above-mentioned trees. The date-palm is highly valued for its fruit and usefulness. Every part of the tree serves a good purpose; nothing of it is wasted. Its fruit, the date, is a nourishing food and the source of date-honey. Its branches are used for shade, for baskets and to make the *lulav*, one (and the "outstanding" one) of the "four species" of the festival of *Succot*, over which a special blessing is recited. Unlike branches of other trees, the branches of the palm are undivided and symbolize oneness with G-d; it also symbolizes victory over the inner adversary, the *Yetzer Hara*.

The cedar of Lebanon is famed for its uprightness, strength and durability. Cedars are evergreen trees, stately in appearance, with a sweet and fresh odor. The wonderful *Bet Hamikdash* built by King Solomon was made from cedars of Lebanon.

For these and other reasons, the *tzaddik* is aptly compared to the date-palm and the cedar of Lebanon.

What the *tzaddik* is among men, the Shabbat is among the days of the week. The *tzaddik* is the perfectly righteous man;

---

66. Ibid. vs. 7-16.

there is no evil in him whatever; he is a thoroughly holy man. Others who have not reached that level are mostly good, but they still have certain traits that have to be improved and perfected. The *tzaddik* is called the "foundation" of the world, for it is in the merit of the *tzaddik* that the world exists, and through him other men are blessed.

Furthermore, Shabbat gives us a "taste" of the World to Come, when all of us will attain the level of *tzaddik*.

Thus, it is significant and meaningful that the hymn to Shabbat should also be a hymn to the *tzaddik*.

According to our Sages, this hymn to the Shabbat (Psalm 92) was composed by none other than Adam himself. Indeed, who could better appreciate the spirit of Shabbat and the spirit of holiness than the first man, the creation of G-d's own hands? If we take time out on Shabbat to reflect upon its significance, in the light of what has been said above, we would be moved to exclaim, with Adam:

> *For You, O G-d have made me rejoice with Your work;*
> *in the works of Your hand I will exult. How great are*
> *Your works, O G-d; Your thoughts are very deep.*

Psalm 92 is followed by Ps. 93, already discussed.[66a] Mourner's Kaddish concludes this part of the service.

כגונא

K'gavna

In *Nusach Ari* the Shabbat hymn (Pss. 92-93) is followed by an excerpt from the *Zohar*[67] (in Aramaic), beginning with the word *K'gavna* ("Just as" or "in the same manner as"). It is a profoundly mystical (i.e., Kabbalistic) passage, and one difficult to explain adequately within the frame of the present volume; all the more so since this is only a small section of a larger context.

66a. *My Prayer*, Vol. I, op. cit. p. 222f.
67. *Zohar* II, *Terumah*, 135a, f.

Nevertheless, inasmuch as it is included in the Siddur and recited in numerous congregations every Friday night, a somewhat free translation will be given here, followed by a brief explanation based on the discourse of the Alter Rebbe, author of the *Tanya,* in the Siddur[68] published by his son and successor, Rabbi Dov Ber Schneuri, the "Mitteler Rebbe."

> *Just as the* [sefirot] *unite Above into One, so, too, does the* [sefirah *of* malchut *(kingship)*] *unite below within the mystery of One, becoming together with them Above — one paralleling one. The Holy One, blessed be He, who is One Above, does not descend upon His Throne of Glory until* [the *sefirah of* malchut] *enters into the mystery of His Oneness to become one in one. This, as has been stated earlier, is the mystical concept of "G-d is One and His Name is One."*[69]

The meaning of this first section of *K'gavna* is as follows:

The six *sefirot* (*chesed, gevurah, tiferet, netzach, hod, yesod*) are united Above, that is, in the realm of *Atzilut,* through the supernal *sefirot chochmah, binah, da'at,* with their Emanator, the *Or Ein Sof* (Infinite Light). In their very source these emanations have no separate identities; they all coalesce there into the perfect oneness of the Infinite Light. It is only when these attributes emanate from their source "downward" into the lower worlds and manifest themselves as definite attributes, that they acquire separate entities in the form of *chesed* (kindness) and *gevurah* (strictness), etc. The significance of this perception is that it helps us understand the principle that "only at their root are the strict judgments sweetened," since there the attribute of *gevurah* (strict judgment) is dissolved into the attribute of *chesed* (kindness) and *rachamim* (mercy), though otherwise these attributes are incompatible.

The "Throne of Glory," in Kabbalistic terms, refers to the seventh *sefirah* — the *sefirah* of *malchut* in the highest of the four

---

68. Vol. II, 14a f. Warsaw 1867.
69. *Zechariah* 14:9. *Zohar II,* Terumah, 135a-b.

supernal worlds, namely, *Atzilut. Malchut* (kingship) is the Divine attribute through which G-d dispenses His creative and benevolent manifestations. In other words, *malchut* is the outlet for the six preceding *sefirot.* The term stems from the metaphor of a human king who rules by fiat or royal decree: "Let it be done." (Thus: G-d *said,* "Let there be...," even though there was as yet nothing and no one to speak to.) "Descending" — or "sitting down" — upon the Throne of Glory" is a figure of speech denoting G-d's "descent" from a state of being unknowable and incomprehensible to a less sublime state of assuming the role of "King" of the *created* order. The analogy from the physical act of sitting down is clear: it entails lowering one's entire stature, including the head. In Kabbalistic terms it denotes G-d's reaching out to His creatures. With benefactor and beneficiary reaching out to each other as much as possible, the two meet and are united as "one into one."

It is on the holy day of Shabbat that the ascent of the lower worlds into the world of *Atzilut* takes place, for this ascent is the result of, and part of the reward for, all the good deeds that have been performed during the preceding six work days. It is there, in the supernal world of *Atzilut,* that the union of the Shechinah with its Source in the Infinite Light is effected. At this point G-d and His Name (where "G-d" refers to the Unknowable Supreme Being and "His Name" refers to the Divine attributes by which G-d can be comprehended to some degree) become one and the same. This, in essence, is the meaning of the expression, "G-d is One and His Name is One."

Bearing the above in mind, we gain a better insight into the second part of *K'gavna*, which, in free translation, reads:

> *The mystery of Shabbat [its most sublime, hidden nature, is as follows]: Shabbat [as said] unites within the mystical One, so that the mystical One may descend upon her during the [Maariv] Prayer of Shabbat night. For [at this time] the Holy Throne* (malchut *of* Atzilut) *unites with the mystical One, elevating her for the descent of the Supreme Holy King upon her. For, as Shab-*

bat was about to arrive, she divested and separated herself from the "other side," and all strict judgments vanished from her. [Thus] she remains (is) in unity with the Holy Light, and crowned herself with many crowns for the Holy King. Thereupon all wrathful powers and adversaries altogether flee from her and vanish, and there is no "other" power to reign in all the worlds. Her countenance lights up with the Supernal Light, and she crowns herself here below, within the holy people; and all are crowned with new souls. Then the prayer brings her [G-d's] blessing with joy and radiant Countenance.

As explained by the Alter Rebbe, the mystery of Shabbat has two dimensions: one is connected with Shabbat night, the other with Shabbat day. The former is conceived in terms of "reflected light" from below — up; the latter is conceived in terms of "direct light" emanating from above — down.

The "reflected light" traveling from below up represents all the good deeds of the past six workdays, each good deed a reflection of the Infinite Light emanating from the Supreme King of the Universe and returning, sublimated, to its Source. As the holy Shabbat arrives on Friday eve and throughout the hours of the night, these lights return to, and are absorbed in, their source in the Infinite Light. Reciprocally, an even greater light from the Infinite Light descends into the lower worlds during the daylight hours of Shabbat. This reciprocal ascent and descent is further stimulated by the special evening and morning prayers of Shabbat. Every Jew participating in the observance of the holy Shabbat receives the special flow of Divine light through the "additional and higher soul" (*neshamah yeteirah*, meaning both an "additional" and "superior" soul). This soul descends and animates the Jew on Shabbat and imbues him and her with *oneg* Shabbat — the special spiritual pleasure of sublime joy and holiness that derives from a closeness to the "radiant countenance" of the Infinite Light.

This is why the Shabbat is said to bring with it a "taste" of *Olam haBa*, the World To Come.

What is the "additional soul" or the "new soul" that animates the Jew on Shabbat?

The Alter Rebbe explains[70] it as follows: The soul, which is a part of G-dliness above, comprises five dimensions or categories: *nefesh, ruach, neshamah, chayah* and *yechidah*. While the soul is incorporeal and cannot be confined entirely within a physical body, it does manifest itself functionally on these levels to various degrees, relative to the degree of spirituality of the individual. The highest and most sublime dimension of the soul, the *yechidah*, only rarely manifests itself in a person on an ordinary day, for it is altogether attached to its source Above. (In the Talmud it is referred to as the *mazzal* of the person.) On Shabbat, however, the *yechidah* of the soul does manifest itself and it irradiates the whole being of the Shabbat observer, and this is the meaning of the words, "and all are crowned with new souls," through which flows "[G-d's] blessing with joy and radiant Countenance." "Radiant Countenance" is the mark of special Divine grace, as in the Priestly Blessing, "May G-d cause His face to shine upon you and be gracious unto you."[71]

סוכת שלום
Succat Shalom

...and spread over us Your tabernacle of peace: Blessed... Who spreads the tabernacle of peace over us, and over His people Israel, and over Jerusalem.

The prayer *Hashkiveinu*,[72] the second blessing after the *Shema*, as it is recited on Friday night, differs from the text recited on the other nights of the week, in two respects. The Friday night

---

70. On the authority of *Etz Chayim*, major source of Lurianic Kabbalah.
71. Numbers 6:25.
72. See *My Prayer*, Vol. I, op. cit., p. 269f.

version (according to *Nusach Ari*) is shorter, having only the beginning of the prayer, up to and not including the words, "and shield us, and remove from us any enemy, pestilence,..." Secondly, the concluding blessing is not, "Blessed...Who guards His people Israel for ever," as during the week, but "...Who spreads the tabernacle of peace over us," etc. In other words, whereas the theme of *Hashkiveinu* on weekdays is "peace and protection," it is only "peace" on Shabbat.

The reason for the change is that on Shabbat the Jewish people require no special protection, because the Shabbat itself protects the Jewish people.[73] When Jews keep the Shabbat, the Shabbat keeps the Jews.

To explain it a little more fully. One of the reasons for the inclusion of *Hashkiveinu* in the Evening Service (*Maariv*) is found in *Midrash Tehillim*. It is based on a saying by Rabbi Eliezer: "He who puts tefillin on his head and arm, *tzitzit* on his garment and a *mezuzah* on his door is guarded against sin."[73a] At night, on weekdays, two of these "guardians" are missing, since the Mitzvot of tefillin and *tzitzit* apply only during daytime. Therefore our Sages included in the Evening Service a special prayer for Divine protection, concluding with a blessing in which G-d is praised as the "Guardian of his people." But since the merit of Shabbat protects the Jewish people, and Shabbat brings peace to every Jew and every Jewish home, the prayer *Hashkiveinu* was shortened and changed accordingly.

The *Kol Bo* suggests a further reason. During the week we pray, "and guard our going out and our coming in," etc. Everyone is then busy coming and going to and from work or business, and everyone therefore requires protection in these comings and goings. On Shabbat and *Yom Tov*, however, which are days of rest, there is no need for this prayer. Our only "business" on Shabbat is to keep it holy. This is why we pray to

---

73. *Abudraham*, based on Midrash and other sources.
73a. *Menachot* 43b.

G-d to spread His tabernacle of peace over us, so that we can indeed observe and honor the Shabbat as it deserves.

According to the *Zohar*, the "tabernacle of peace" (*succat-shalom*) refers to the "extra soul" (*neshama yeteira*), that imbues every Jew when Shabbat comes, and departs with the *Havdalah* at the termination of Shabbat. Our praying, "spread over us Your tabernacle of peace," is an expression of our being prepared and eager to receive this holy experience. The *Zohar* declares:

> *At that moment* [when the Jews recite this prayer], the Divine Shechinah *radiates its light and spreads its wings over the world, and every Jew receives an additional soul, and with it all sadness and sorrow is forgotten, and only joy pervades the Upper and Lower worlds.*[74]

According to the saintly *Ari*, it is necessary to rise to one's feet when reciting this blessing, as a sign of respect for the Divine *Shechinah*.

Elsewhere the *Zohar* states:

> *When the holy day begins on the eve of Shabbat, the tabernacle of peace descends and spreads over the world. What is this "tabernacle of peace"? This is the Shabbat.... For this reason we recite the blessing, "Who spreads the tabernacle of peace over us, and over all His people Israel, and over Jerusalem." Why "over Jerusalem"? Because that is the dwelling-place of the Tabernacle. And it is necessary to welcome this "succah," that it spread over us, and dwell with us and protect us, like a mother hovering over her young so that they have no fear from any side.*
>
> *When the Jewish people bless and welcome this tabernacle of peace and say, "Who spreads a tabernacle of peace," a great holiness descends from On High and spreads its wings over the people of Israel and shelters them, like a mother sheltering her young; and all evil*

---

74. *Zohar* II, *Vayakhel* 205a.

*things depart from the world, and Israel dwells under
the holiness of their Divine Master and they receive new
souls from this tabernacle of peace.... Said Rabbi
Shimon, It is in reference to this that it has been taught
that Shabbat is a taste of the World to Come.*[75]

In this connection, the *Zohar* goes on to explain the significance of lighting the Shabbat candles, symbolizing the sacred light that radiates from the Divine *Shechinah*, the "tabernacle of peace," and why this great Mitzvah was given as a special privilege to the Jewish woman. For, while it is true that the reason is because Chava (Eve) extinguished the light of the world (by causing death, etc.,), there is a deeper significance and mystery. For the "tabernacle of peace" personifies the "Mistress of the world," the Source of the souls called the "candles of G-d." For this reason, it was to the "mistress of the home" that the Mitzvah of candle-lighting was given. "She should, therefore, light the candles with gladness of heart and with joy, for it is a great honor to her, and a great *zechut*, in the merit of which she will be blessed with holy children that will be like shining candles with their Torah and piety, bringing peace to the world; and her husband will be blessed with long life. This is why she should be most careful to observe the Mitzvah of candle-lighting...."[76]

עמידה
The Amidah

The *Amidah* of Shabbat as well as of the festivals begins and concludes with the same three blessings that open and close the weekday's *Shemone Esrei* (eighteen benedictions). We need not therefore, talk about these six blessings here.[1] The intermediate

---

75. *Zohar* I, *Bereishit* 48a.
76. Ibid. 48b.
1. See *My Prayer*, Vol. I op. cit. p. 172f.

thirteen blessings of the weekday *Shemone Esrei* are not said on
Shabbat and *Yom Tov*, for these blessings express our daily
needs and requests; they are connected with mundane worries
and desires, and have no place in the prayers of Shabbat and
Yom Tov, which are days of holiness and serene joy. Instead of
the thirteen blessings we have only one blessing, which is called
"*Kedushat ha-yom*," the blessing that speaks of "the holiness of
the day." Thus we have only seven blessings in the *Amidah* of
Kabbalat Shabbat (as also in the morning, *Musaf* and afternoon
services). This *Amidah* is called "*Tefilat Sheva*," the prayer of
seven (blessings).

Our Sages find a hint for the seven blessings in Psalm 29
(*Mizmor l'David*), which is said on Shabbat (earlier in the *Kabbalat* Shabbat service).[2] In this Psalm the "voice of G-d" is mentioned seven times, reflecting the seven forms of Divine
revelation at Mount Sinai, by which the children of Israel perceived the voice of G-d. Besides, Shabbat is the seventh day, and
is the source of blessing for all the seven days of the week. Hence
it is quite appropriate to recite seven blessings in the *Amidah,* all
of which are devoted to the glorification of G-d's Name.

Let us now consider the blessing of "*Kedushat ha-Yom.*"

אתה קדשת

Atah Kidashta

You have sanctified the Seventh Day unto Your Name,
As the purpose of the creation of heaven and earth;
You blessed it above all days and sanctified it above all
seasons;
And thus it is written in Your Torah:

This is a form of introduction to the quotation from the Torah
where the Shabbat was first instituted. The words, "You sancti-

---

2. See p. 24 above.

fied the Seventh Day... You blessed it...'' are in direct reference to the passage in the Torah, *Vayechulu*, where it is stated that "G-d blessed the Seventh Day and sanctified it."[3] It would have been proper, therefore, to begin this prayer in the same order: "You blessed the Seventh Day and sanctified it...." But apparently the Sages of the Great Assembly who formulated the text of our prayers wished to emphasize the *holiness* of Shabbat, at the same time alluding to the word *kiddushin*, "betrothal." G-d betrothed, so to speak, the Shabbat to the Jewish people. The Jewish people and the Shabbat are "married," as it were, to each other, and no other nation has any part in the holiness of the Shabbat, like a husband and wife who belong to each other and no other person can have a share in their married life.

What does it mean in practical terms — that G-d sanctified the Shabbat unto His Name? It means that the Shabbat is more than a rest day, when man is to rest from his physical work; nor is it a day merely for socializing, or for ordinary enjoyment and recreation with the family. It has a higher purpose; it is different from all days and seasons. It is a day of holiness, of prayer and of study of the Torah. It is dedicated to G-d. Thus it brings a complete change from everyday life, as we had occasion to discuss elsewhere.[4] Shabbat is holier than any other day of the year, and desecration of the Shabbat is a graver sin than even desecration of the Day of Atonement. On the Shabbat, when properly observed, the Jew reaches the highest degree of completeness that any creature of G-d can ever reach. That is why the Shabbat is the end and purpose of the entire Creation, for when man reaches that height, he "justifies" the Creation, and G-d is pleased with His great handiwork. That is also why the Shabbat was especially blessed, and it holds the key of blessings for each and every day of the week. When the Shabbat is properly observed, not only is the Jew blessed spiritually and mentally

---

3. Genesis 2:3.
4. See p. 46 above, on Psalm 92.

and is a happy and contented man during the week, but he is also blessed materially, and whatever he earns during the week is blessed so that he can spend it on good things, on happy things, and not on sickness bills, G-d forbid, or the like. The true measure of "prosperity" is not in the amount of money one earns during the week, but in the way that money is spent and used.

It is the purpose of the work of Creation.

The Shabbat was created last, not because it is least important but, on the contrary, because it was the end purpose of all Creation. This was already mentioned in the hymn of *Lecha Dodi*, in the words, "last in Creation, first in design (thought)."[5]

What is meant by "end purpose of Creation" is this: G-d created the world and all creatures out of His pure goodness, in order to be good to them. The most important creature on earth is, of course, the human creature. Now, the greatest good, and the greatest pleasure, for humans is not eating and drinking, like animals, but to know G-d and to serve Him with all heart and soul. During the week it is difficult to enjoy this closeness to G-d in the fullest measure. The greatest pleasure comes on Shabbat, which is totally dedicated to G-d, without distraction of any kind of work, anxiety and the like. This is why we speak of *oneg Shabbat*, the "delight of Shabbat." Indeed, our Sages declare that the Shabbat is "like one-sixtieth of *Olam Haba* (the World to Come)."[6] It is just a "taste," as it were, of *Olam Haba*, where the pure souls enjoy the nearness of G-d all the time. In this world, while the soul is housed in a body, we are simply incapable of absorbing such sublime and eternal blissfulness, but on Shabbat we get a "smacking" of it. This is why the Shabbat is the end purpose of Creation, for it is on Shabbat that a Jew and the entire Creation, attain the highest and most complete fulfilment in the closest reunion between Creator and created.

---

5. See p. 32.
6. *Berachot* 57b.

You blessed it above all days, and sanctified it above all seasons.

In addition to blessing the Shabbat at the time of Creation, G-d blessed it again in a way that made it quite obvious to the Jewish people. This was when the manna began coming down from Heaven on the 31st day (16th day of Iyar) after the exodus from Egypt. Each day, the Torah tells us, the manna came down and the people scattered around the camp to gather it. And whether one gathered much or little, when they measured it there was exactly one measure (an *omer,* or tenth of an *ephah*), for each person. On Friday they discovered that everyone received a double portion, and they were told by Mosheh *Rabbeinu* that the extra portion was for Shabbat, since there would be no manna coming down from Heaven on the holy day, and all preparations for Shabbat had to be made on the day before Shabbat.[7] (This is one reason why we have two loaves for each meal of Shabbat, called *lechem mishneh.*) Thus, G-d blessed the Shabbat with manna, and every Shabbat ever since; so that no Jew should have to work on the holy Shabbat day, because G-d sends His blessing before Shabbat.

Being "blessed above all days" means, according to the holy *Zohar,* that G-d blessed the holy Shabbat to make it the *source* of blessings for all the days of the week. Each day of the week receives its blessings from the holy Shabbat. This is what the author of *Lecha Dodi* refers to in saying that the Shabbat is the "source of blessing," as mentioned above.[8]

Being "sanctified above all seasons" means being holier than any other festival in the Jewish calendar. Every *Yom Tov* is holy, but Shabbat is holier, for there are levels of holiness in time, space and persons. This is the reason why we make *Havdalah* also when Shabbat is immediately followed by *Yom Tov,* though we conclude the *Havdalah* with the words: *hamavdil bein kodesh*

---

7. Exodus 16:22-27.
8. See p. 32.

l'kodesh ("Who separates holy from holy") instead of *bein kodesh l'chol* ("between holy and profane"). For this reason also, if *Yom Tov* is on a Friday, we must not prepare from *Yom Tov* for Shabbat, unless we make an *eiruv tavshillin* on erev *Yom Tov*, and the preparation is then considered an extension of what has been started on erev *Yom Tov*.

ויכלו

Vayechulu

And the heaven and the earth were finished and all their host. [9]

The "host" of the heavens are all the stars and planets, and the "host" of the earth are all the creatures, including water, soil, grass, trees, etc.

And G-d finished by the Seventh Day His work which He had made, and rested (better: stopped*) on the Seventh Day from all His work which He had made.* [10]

As the great interpreter of the Torah, *Rashi*, explains, mortal man cannot know the time exactly; this is one of the reasons why we usher in the Shabbat 18-20 minutes before sunset. But G-d knows the time exactly, and He finished His work *"by* the Seventh Day," and stopped from all His work. G-d does not have to "rest," for He never gets tired. Although *Shabbat* (from the words *vayishbot* and *shavat*) in this portion is translated "a day of rest," it really means a day of *stoppage*, stoppage from all manner of "work." The Hebrew word used here in the Torah is not *avodah*, which is work, in the sense of any kind of labor that requires a physical effort; the word here is *melachah*, which has quite a different meaning, and includes also *acts* which require no effort. To strike a match, or turn the electric switch, requires

---

9. Genesis 2:1.
10. Ibid., v. 2.

no effort, yet it is forbidden on the Shabbat just like tilling the soil, or bricklaying, as mentioned earlier.[10a]

It is interesting to note that in the beginning of this portion we find the expression "...*were* finished" (*vayechulu*), but then we find the expression "And *G-d* finished" (*vayechal*). The first gives us the idea that the heaven and earth and all their hosts "were finished" by the word of G-d; G-d spoke, and the world came into being. The second time the idea is given that G-d put the finishing touches, so to speak, on everything He created; He introduced the laws of nature and complete harmony in the entire universe. It is also interesting to note that *vayechal* has also the meaning of "and he *desired*," as indeed it is translated in *Targum Yerushalmi*. Thus, the meaning would be, "and G-d desired the Seventh Day." That is why Shabbat is called *Chemdat Yamim* (the "desirable of days").

> *And G-d blessed the Seventh Day and made it holy, for on it He rested (stopped) from all His work, which G-d had created and made (to make).*[11]

G-d blessed the Seventh Say itself; G-d had already blessed the creatures, and now He blessed the Shabbat, and made it the source of blessing for all days of the week.

The words "created to make" are explained to mean "to continue making," that is to say, that G-d's acts of creation never really stopped, but that He continually creates everything, and keeps everything in existence, so that they would not become non-existent again, as they were before G-d created them. Although nature seems to continue on its own by the laws of nature, it is really G-d the Creator who constantly makes these laws work, so that the process of creation goes on continuously.

An additional meaning is given to these words by our Sages. "To make" also refers to man. G-d *created* everything from nothing, but man was given the power to *make* things, and to use

---

10a. See p. 46 f.; also p. 136 below.
11. Gen. 2, v. 3.

the forces of nature to develop and improve the conditions of life. Man has been made "a partner" in Creation. If he lives according to the laws of G-d, he can make the world a better place to live in; but he also has the power to destroy things. This "partnership" was given to man together with the Shabbat, for the Shabbat is a "memorial of the Creation." When we observe the Shabbat properly, we are living witnesses who testify by our way of life that G-d is the Creator; we recognize the supreme majesty of G-d, and we try to be good "partners" helping to build, and not to destroy, the world. This is what was meant when the great sage Rav Hamnuna said:

> *"He who prays on the eve of Shabbat and says* Vaye-chulu, *is regarded by the Torah as if he has been made a partner in the Creation."*[12]

The importance of reciting *Vayechulu* in the *Amidah* of Friday night is further underscored in the Talmud where it is stated: "Said Rav, or possibly Rabbi Yehoshua ben Levi, 'Even a person praying individually on Friday eve has to recite *Vaye-chulu.*'" Further on: "Mar Ukva said, 'When a person recites *Vayechulu* in the Friday eve prayer, the two angels accompanying him place their hands on his head and say, 'Your sin is departed and your transgression is forgiven.'"[13]

Of course, the Talmud does not speak of one who recites words without concentrating his mind and heart on their meaning. Such a person would hardly be worthy of being considered a "partner with G-d in Creation," or deserve to have his sins and transgressions forgiven. It is only when the person really concentrates on these significant three verses of the Torah that sum up the Creation account, expresses his deep conviction that G-d is the Creator of the heaven and the earth and all their hosts, and actually shows by his devotion to the holy Shabbat and its fullest

---

12. *Shabbat* 119b.
13. Ibid.

observance that his whole life is guided by this truth, that he can
be considered G-d's partner in the Creation.

Declares the *Zohar*:

By reciting this portion from the Torah, a Jew gives testimony
that G-d created the heaven and the earth and all that is in them
in six days, and rested on the seventh day, which He proclaimed
a holy day of rest. The Jewish people are the living witnesses that
attest to this truth, and every Jew should realize the great and
unique privilege to be such a witness. Hence the *Zohar* concludes: "A Jew should give this testimony with joy and gladness
of heart."[14]

This is also one of the reasons why *Vayechulu* is recited not
only in the silent *Amidah*, but is repeated again, and aloud,
immediately after the *Amidah*. It should also be said standing,
because witnesses giving testimony in a (Jewish) court do so
standing, as also explained by the *Abudraham* and other
authorities.

Another reason is that when *Yom Tov* occurs on Shabbat, the
Yom Tov Amidah which is said on Friday night, does not contain *Vayechulu*. The Sages therefore instituted to say *Vayechulu*
after the *Amidah*, and made it the rule to recite it after the
Amidah on all Friday nights.

ישמחו

Yismechu

Because *Vayechulu* is to be recited with profound joy, as mentioned above, the short prayer following it — *Yismechu* — is
especially fitting. It reads:

> Let them rejoice with Your Kingdom they who observe
> the Shabbat and call it a delight, (namely) the nation
> which sanctifies the Seventh Day; they shall all be

---

14. *Zohar, Vayakhel* 207b; *Tur* par. 268.

satiated and gratified with Your goodness. You took pleasure in the Seventh Day and made it holy; You called it 'most desirable of days,' in remembrance of the work of Creation.

In general it may be said that this prayer is almost like a paraphrase of *Vayechulu.* The wording of it, however, as in all prayers, is carefully chosen and meaningful.

Rejoicing (*simchah*) is usually associated with our festivals, but it also applies to Shabbat. Indeed, the Abudraham points to the verse, "And in the day of your rejoicing and festivals,"[15] noting the commentary of the *Sifri* to the effect that "in the day of your rejoicing" refers to Shabbat.

It is they who "observe Shabbat" that can truly rejoice in G-d's Kingdom, since the observance of Shabbat, which testifies to G-d's creation of the world, testifies at the same time to His Kingdom, for the Creator of the world is also its King and Master. And realizing who our King and Master is, we can truly rejoice in His Kingdom.

Observing the Shabbat and keeping it holy brings us the sure promise of being satiated — gratified *to the fullest* — with G-d's goodness, both in this world and in the World To Come.

G-d "desired" the Seventh Day and called it "Desirable of Days." This means that while the Six Days of Creation were necessary to create the world, it is the Seventh Day that G-d really desired and made holy.

In our life, too, living as we are in a material world, we are expected to work and toil during the six days of the week, but these days are not an end in themselves; they are but a means to attain a higher form of living, to rise to a state of holiness, which is personified by the Shabbat. Throughout the six days of the week Jews live for, and look forward to, the holy Shabbat — just as our entire life on this earth is a preparation for the eternal life.

---

15. Numbers 10:10.

אלקינו...רצה נא במנוחתנו
Elokeinu...Retzei Na Bimnuchateinu

The next section of the Friday night *Amidah* is a prayer in which we ask G-d to accept with favor our Shabbat rest, to sanctify us with His commandments and grant us a portion in His Torah; to satiate us with His goodness, gladden our soul with His salvation and purify our heart to serve Him in truth; and to lovingly and graciously cause us to inherit the holy Shabbat so that all Israel (the Jewish people) who sanctify G-d's Name will find rest on it. The prayer is concluded with the blessing: "Blessed... who sanctifies the Shabbat."

Examining carefully the text of this prayer, we can see that it refers to both the "passive" and "active" aspects of Shabbat. As a day of rest from all work, we observe it simply by not doing any of the forbidden 39 kinds of work and their offshoots. This is the so-called "passive" aspect of Shabbat, and is referred to in this prayer by the words "accept with favor our (Shabbat) rest." At the same time, Shabbat has its "active" aspect, in that it is dedicated to Mitzvot and the study of Torah. This is why the prayer continues with the words "sanctify us with Your commandments and grant us a portion in Your Torah."

"Grant us a portion in Your Torah" refers to the fact that every Jew has a portion and share in the Torah. It is impossible for every person to study and master the *whole* Torah, but no matter what the level of understanding is, one has a portion in the Torah. By studying Torah every day to the best of one's ability, one takes possession of one's very own "share" in the Torah. In this way, all Jews collectively share in the *whole* Torah.

"Satiate us with Your goodness...Your salvation" is a prayer for G-d's direct benevolence and salvation, without intermediaries.

"Purify our heart" means that we ask G-d's help to serve Him wholeheartedly and sincerely, without any thought of reward.

"Lovingly and graciously cause us to inherit Your holy Shabbat." The words *b'ahava u'bratzon* — "with love and favor" — are a keynote of Shabbat, and they occur in the prayers, as well as in the *Kiddush*, on Friday night. They remind us that when the Shabbat was first given to the Jewish people, even before they received the Torah, it was given with love and favor. For when the manna came down from Heaven thirty days after the liberation from Egypt, a double portion came down on the day before Shabbat so they did not need to collect it on the holy Shabbat. This showed them plainly how lovingly and graciously G-d took care of their needs for the Shabbat, and what a wonderful gift the Shabbat was.

According to some authorities, the concluding words of this prayer also refer to the "eternal Shabbat" in the World to Come. We pray to G-d that just as He first gave us the Shabbat with love and favor, so may He cause us and all children of Israel to inherit eternal life and rest in the World to Come.

The concluding blessing, "Who sanctifies the Shabbat," differs from the text of the blessing which we say on *Yom Tov*, which includes also the word "Israel," thus: "Who sanctifies Israel and the Festivals" (if the festival occurs on Shabbat, "Who sanctifies the Shabbat and Israel and the Festivals"; on *Rosh Hashanah* and *Yom Kippur*, the name of the festival is mentioned explicitly).

According to the *Abudraham* (quoting the tractate *Sofrim*), there is a significant reason why the word "Israel" is left out of the blessing on Shabbat. This is due to the fact that G-d Himself sanctified the Shabbat at the time of Creation, when there was not yet a Jewish people in existence to observe the Shabbat and keep it holy. On the other hand, the festivals were given already after the Jewish people became a nation and had been given the Torah. Moreover, the actual timing of the festivals was entrusted to the Jewish people, through the *Bet Din* (High Court). Thus, for example, the Torah says that the first day of Passover is on the fifteenth of the first month (*Nissan*), but it was the *Bet Din* who had the authority to determine and sanctify the New Moon (*Rosh Chodesh*), that is, the first day of each month. It could also put in an extra whole month before *Nissan* (*Adar Sheni*) to make it a leap year if it found it necessary to do so. It follows that the final word as to when each festival should begin was left to the *Bet Din* (eventually a permanent calendar was fixed, which we use to this day).[16] Thus the festivals are sanctified — by Divine authority — through Israel, while the Shabbat has been sanctified independently from the Seventh Day of Creation by G-d Himself.

ברכה אחת מעין שבע
One Blessing Containing Seven

During the evening service there is usually no repetition of the silent *Amidah* by the *Chazzan*, as during the morning and afternoon prayers. On Friday night, however, there is an exception in that an abbreviated form of the *Amidah* is repeated by the *Chazzan*, namely, the "One Blessing Containing Seven." The seven blessings are, of course, the three opening blessings and three closing blessings common to all *Amidahs*, with the central blessing referring to the holy Shabbat.

This seven-fold blessing begins like the first blessing of all *Amidahs*, but ends with the words "Master of heaven and earth." It then continues with the prayer *Magen avot* ("Shield of Our Fathers"), which is recited first by the congregation and then by the *Chazzan*, followed by *Elokeinu...retzei na bimnuchateinu*, concluding with the blessing, "Blessed...Who sanctifies the Shabbat." Thus, it is a so-called "long" blessing, beginning and ending with a blessing.

The words "Master of Heaven and earth" are self-explanatory, for they refer to the fact that by Friday night, the

---

16. About the Jewish Calendar see p. 157 below.

Six Days of Creation came to an end, whereupon the Creator
became in actuality the Master of all that He created.

It is in the prayer *Magen avot* that the seven blessings are
specifically mentioned, as we shall see later.

There are various reasons why an exception was made in the
Friday night service in the form of the seven-fold blessing. In the
Talmud[17] the reason given is that of security. According to
Rashi, the evening service was, in those days, usually recited at
home because it was dangerous to go out at night. After returning from work towards the evening, everyone stayed indoors and
recited the *Maariv* prayer at home. On Friday night, however, in
honor of the Shabbat, the people gathered in the synagogue
(which was usually on the outskirts of the town). Now, for the
sake of some individuals who might be a little late in coming to
Shul, the Friday night service was extended with the addition of
the seven-fold blessing, so that all worshipers (including the
latecomers) could leave the synagogue together to go home.

It should be added that, whenever a reason is given for any
prayer or Mitzvah, it is not the *only* reason, nor necessarily the
primary reason. Such reason, or reasons, are in most cases
"external" explanations. The most important reason is the
prayer, or Mitzvah, itself, each one having its own deep, inner
and hidden significance, derived from, and rooted in, G-dliness.
Our Sages and Kabbalists (especially in the *Zohar*, and in the
writings of the saintly *Ari*, Rabbi Yitzchak Luria) have given us
some glimpses into the deep mysteries of our prayers and Mitzvot, but even these are mere glimpses. Some of them we have
endeavored to include in this modest commentary, and then
only in their simplest aspects.

Now, for a better understanding of the seven-fold blessing, let
us look into the text.

---

17. *Shabbat* 24b.

מגן אבות
Magen Avot

He was a shield of our fathers with His word, He revives the dead by His utterance, He is the holy G-d (on Shabbat-Teshuvah substitute: the holy King), like whom there is none; He gives rest to His people on His holy Shabbat day, for in them He took pleasure to give them rest — Him we shall serve with awe and trembling, and offer thanks to His Name every day, continually, according to its blessings. He is the G-d worthy of thanks, Master of peace, who sanctifies the Shabbat and blesses the Seventh Day, and brings rest with holiness to a people satiated with delight — in remembrance of the work of Creation.

The words "Shield of Our Fathers," "He revives the dead" and "the holy G-d" clearly refer to the familiar first three blessings of all *Amidahs*. The words "He gives rest to His people on His holy Shabbat" refer to the central Shabbat blessing *retze bimnuchateinu* ("accept favorably our rest") explained earlier. The words "before Him we shall worship," "G-d of praise" and "Master of Peace" clearly refer to the familiar last three blessings of every *Amidah*.

The prayer *Magen avot* concludes with the words "a remembrance to the work of Creation." This, of course, refers to the fact that our first testimony in observing Shabbat is to acknowledge and give expression to the basic truth that G-d is the Creator of the universe. This is stated in the fourth of the Ten Commandments: "Remember the Shabbat day to keep it holy... for in six days G-d made heaven and earth...."[18] To be sure, Shabbat is also a memorial to *Yetziat Mitzraim*, the exodus from Egypt, as stated in the repetition of the Ten Commandments.[19]

---

18. Exodus 20:8.
19. Deuteronomy 5:12.

But in the Friday night prayer we emphasize the first aspect of Shabbat, which came before *Yetziat Mitzraim*. Later on, in *Kiddush*, we mention both aspects of Shabbat, namely, as a memorial to Creation and also as a memorial to *Yetziat Mitzraim*. (In *Kiddush* on *Yom Tov* we mention only *Yetziat Mitzraim*, because the festivals, especially *Pesach*, *Shavuot* and *Succot*, are connected with *Yetziat Mitzraim*, and not directly with the Creation).

It is significant, of course, that each of the silent *Amidot* of Shabbat (evening, morning, *Musaf*, and *Minchah*) contains *seven* blessings (instead of eighteen — actually nineteen — on weekdays, for example). Shabbat is the *seventh* day of Creation, which G-d made holy. Moreover, the entire Creation came into being through the seven Divine attributes (from *Chesed*, kindness, through *Malchut*, royalty), as explained at length in Kabbalah and Chassidut. Indeed, Shabbat incorporates all seven Divine attributes, all blended into perfect harmony and peace, one more reason why Shabbat is the embodiment of peace and holy rest, as noted in the holy *Zohar*.[20]

ה' רועי

Psalm 23: HaShem Ro'ee

According to *Nusach Ari*, the order of the Friday night service, following the *Kaddish-shalem* after the "seven-fold blessing" calls for the recital of Psalm 23 by the entire congregation, after which the *Chazzan* recites the *Half-Kaddish* and *Barchu*, to which the congregation responds. The *Kabbalat* Shabbat service is then concluded with *Aleinu*.

Psalm 23 is one of the most familiar of *Tehillim*. It is also one of the most beautiful and comforting. That it has a special significance for Shabbat can be seen from the fact that it is not only

---

20. *Zohar, Ber.* 480a f.

included in the *Kabbalat* Shabbat service, but is also said before *Kiddush* — both on Friday night and before the second Shabbat meal on Shabbat day. Also at the *Seudah Shelishit,* wherever *zmirot* are chanted, it is almost invariably the first. The connection between this psalm and Shabbat will be pointed out later. First, let us understand what King David tells us in this beautiful psalm.

> *G-d is my shepherd, I shall not lack* (be short of anything).[21]

From the story of his life, which is described in the Book of Samuel, we know that David started his eventful life as a shepherd. He was a faithful shepherd, who loved his flocks, took care of their needs and protected them against all predators. It was therefore quite natural for him to describe G-d's love and protection in terms of a "shepherd," as he does also in other psalms. But King David was not the first to call G-d "shepherd." Our father Jacob already spoke of G-d as having been his "shepherd" all his life.[22] He, too, like all our Patriarchs, was a shepherd. And so the idea of G-d being our shepherd came down also through our prophets.

> *He makes me lie down in green pastures; He leads me beside still waters.*[23]

Like a lamb under the protection of a faithful shepherd, David feels secure and serene under the loving care of the Divine Shepherd.

David does not speak here only of mere food and water. Men of spirit, saintly men, do not consider the material aspects of life as the most important things in life. These are necessary, of course, but bare necessities are all they require. If they speak of food, clothing and shelter (the three basic human needs), they

---

21. Psalms 23:1.
22. Genesis 48:15.
23. Psalms 23:2.

have in mind the spiritual "food, clothing and shelter" of the
soul, and these, for a Jew, are the Torah and Mitzvot. This is
more clearly indicated in the next verse:

> *He restores my soul; He guides me in the paths of right-*
> *eousness for His Name's sake.*[24]

Recalling how often his life was in danger — he fought a lion
and a bear, the Philistine giant Goliath; he dodged the sword of
King Saul who was crazed by jealousy; he faced hunger and
thirst in the desert, he fought many battles on behalf of his
people — David proclaims his steadfast faith and trust in G-d,
as he expresses it so beautifully in the following verse:

> *Even if I walk in the valley of the shadow of death, I*
> *shall fear no evil, for You are with me. Your rod and*
> *your staff, they comfort me.*[25]

G-d does not spare the "rod" of painful discipline when this
is necessary for the benefit of a person, but there is always His
"staff" to lean on, and both are a source of comfort to the
believer, since they bring him closer to G-d.

> *You prepare a table before me in the presence of my*
> *enemies; You have anointed my head with oil; my cup*
> *runs over.*[26]

Here King David refers to his final victory over all his enemies
and to his highest achievement — being chosen by G-d to
become King of the Jewish people. Truly his reward was complete and more. Yet it was not the crown that brought him the
greatest satisfaction, but the "goodness and loving-kindness"
with which he filled all the days of his life. But there was one
unfulfilled wish: To build the House of G-d, the *Bet Hamikdash*,
which was not given to him, but to his son, King Shlomo

---

24. Ibid., v. 3.
25. Ibid., v. 4.
26. Ibid., v. 5.

(Solomon). These deep feelings he expresses in the concluding verse:

> *Only goodness and loving-kindness will follow me all the days of my life, and I will dwell in the House of G-d for many long years.*[27]

*   *   *

What has been said above in explaining the psalm is the "plain" meaning of it. We must remember that *Tehillim*, as a part of the Torah, has more than one meaning, and there are at least four basic levels of interpretation of the Torah: *pshat* (plain meaning), *remez* (hidden meaning), *drash* (allegorical teaching, by way of "images," as in a parable) and *sod* (deep mystical meaning). All these are found also in this psalm, some of which will be mentioned here briefly.

Our Sages tell us that King David in his Book of Psalms did not speak only of himself or for himself, but he spoke for and on behalf of all Jewish people and for every Jew individually. His personal experiences reflect very closely the experience of the Jewish people as a whole. This is especially true in this particular psalm, in which our Sages see a true image of the birth of our Jewish nation, from its miraculous liberation from Egyptian bondage, to receiving the Torah at Sinai, and through the forty years' wandering in the desert on the way to the Promised Land. Throughout this critical period (as also through our long Jewish history), G-d has been our faithful shepherd, taking care of all needs, material and spiritual.

The "green pastures" and "still waters," our Sages tell us,[28] refer to the wonderful way in which G-d made the desert flourish for our wandering ancestors. The miraculous well that flowed from a rock accompanying our ancestors in the desert, not only provided them with refreshing water, but also caused green pastures to flourish around them wherever they encamped, filling

---

27. Ibid., v. 6.
28. *Yalkut* on *Tehillim*.

the air and their very clothes with refreshing fragrance. These green pastures also helped sustain the large flocks of sheep and herds of cattle that they took with them from Egypt.

"He restores my soul…, the Midrash says, refers to the Giving of the Torah, as it is written, "G-d's Torah is perfect; it restores the soul."[29] It is the sustaining and vitalizing life force of the Jewish soul, its very "food and water." There is an allusion in this verse also to the "quails" (*slav*) and the Clouds of Glory with which G-d so graciously protected our ancestors in the desert, not always because of their merits, but "for His Name's sake," so that they and, indeed, all mankind would recognize the greatness of G-d's Name and the wonders of Divine Providence.

In the same vein the *Midrash* explains the words "valley of the shadow of death" as referring to the perils of the desert, with its poisonous snakes and scorpions, as well as marauding tribes, that would have made life unbearable for our ancestors but for G-d's loving care. Thus, they marched on without fear, knowing that the pillar of fire moving ahead of them cleared their path of all dangers. There were those who, from time to time, provoked G-d's anger, and the "rod" came down swiftly, but there was always the "staff" to lean on by returning to G-d and His Torah.

"You prepare a table before me…, the *Midrash*[30] observes, refers to the manna, which piled up high as a table around them, so that they would not have to exert themself picking it from the ground. In this way G-d confounded the hopes of Israel's enemies, who had expected them to perish in the desert. This was the answer to the challenge, "Could G-d prepare a table in the desert?"[31]

King David, the Jewish people as a whole and every Jew individually yearn for "goodness" (*tov*) and "loving-kindness"

29. Psalms 19:8.
30. *Shemot Rabbah Beshallach,* 25:8.
31. Psalms 78:19.

(chesed), which refer to the Torah, a "good doctrine" (Lekach tov) and a "Torah of loving-kindness" (Torat chesed).

Now, where is the connection between Psalm 23 and Shabbat?

There are several points that can be mentioned here. First, the whole serene picture of peace and comfort, free from anxiety and fear, and a feeling of nearness to G-d — all this reflects the Shabbat atmosphere and Shabbat feeling which the Shabbat observer feels in this Divinely blessed and sanctified day.

Further, this psalm is sometimes called the "parnasah psalm," for it reminds us that G-d is our true provider, our shepherd. The holy Shabbat day is also, in a very real sense, the "shepherd" of the entire week in light of what our Sages told about Shabbat being the source of blessings for all the other six days of the week, both materially and spiritually.

In a still deeper sense, on the mystical level, the holy Zohar,[32] commenting on the last verse of the psalm, explains that both "goodness" (tov) and "loving-kindness" (chesed) refer to G-d, Who is the source of both. What, then, is tov and what is chesed? Tov refers to the kind of good that may come down from G-d also in a hidden form, while chesed is the obvious kind of benevolence that G-d bestows freely on His creatures, even the undeserving. We mention both kinds in our Grace After Meals, in which we express our gratitude to G-d "Who feeds the whole world in His goodness, kindness and benevolence." On the holy Shabbat, the Zohar goes on, even the hidden spiritual good, the highest of all, comes down to us in a revealed perception, well within our feeling and experience. This is why the Shabbat hymn Mizmor shir l'yom haShabbat (Psalm 92) begins with the word tov — "It is good to give thanks to G-d" — and Psalm 23, which is also closely identified with the Shabbat, concludes with tov — "only goodness and loving-kindness will follow me all the days of my life."

---

32. Terumah, 168b.

RETURNING HOME FROM SHUL ON FRIDAY EVE

מלאכי השלום
Angels of Peace

Our Sages of the Talmud tell us:

Two angels accompany every Jew coming home from *shul* on the eve of Shabbat: a good angel and a bad angel. Upon entering the home and finding the candles burning, the table set and the house filled with the beauty and peace of the Shabbat spirit, the good angel says, "May it be like this also next Shabbat!" and the bad angel begrudgingly says, "Amen!" However, if the house is found unprepared for Shabbat, with all those beautiful things missing, the bad angel says, "May it be like this next Shabbat also!" and the good angel unwillingly says "Amen!"[1]

Quoting this Talmudic source, the *Tur*[2] and *Shulchan Aruch* emphasize the importance of the final preparations of the home in honor of the Shabbat Queen, namely, setting the Shabbat table.

Since the Shabbat candles must be lit in good time (not less than 18-20 minutes) before sunset, the table is set before that time. A spotless Shabbat cloth is spread over the table, with two *challot* loaves placed at its head (and for other males of the family, as well as for guests, if any). The *challot* loaves are covered with a cloth. One of the reasons for the *two* loaves — called *lechem mishneh*, "double bread," is to remind us of the double portion of manna which came down on Friday for Shabbat also. For the same reason the *challot* are covered, because

---

1. *Shabbat* 119b.
2. *Orach Chayim*, par. 262.

78

the manna came down on a layer of dew and was covered with dew to keep it fresh, as our Sages tell us. Another reason for covering the *challot* is in order not to "shame" them when *Kiddush* is recited over wine.

Afer the *challot* are placed on the table and covered with a Shabbat cloth, the candles are set and lit by the mother and daughters, having first dressed in their Shabbat dresses, just as the men put on their Shabbat clothes, in honor of Shabbat. After lighting the candles, the women cover their faces and recite the blessing, "Who sanctified us with His commandments and commanded us to kindle the light of the holy Shabbat."

The reason for covering the face while reciting the blessing is this: A blessing has to be recited in every case *before* performing the Mitzvah. In the present case, if the blessing were said first and the holy Shabbat ushered in thereby, lighting the candles would be a desecration of Shabbat. Therefore, the candles must be lit first. Covering the face hides them from view, while the blessing is recited, and then seeing them for the first time as the sacred lights of Shabbat after the blessing has been recited, is equivalent to having made the blessing before the Mitzvah. This is also a good time for the mother to whisper a personal prayer that G-d bless her home and household, her husband and children, with good health and happiness, and true *Yiddishe nachas*.

It is also customary for the women and girls to place some money in a charity box for *tzedakah, before* the candle lighting ceremony.

Thus, when the husband and children return home from *shul* on Friday eve, accompanied by the angels, they find the heartwarming and blissful Shabbat atmosphere, and all the members of the family greet each other affectionately with "Shabbat Shalom!" to the delight of the accompanying angels.

In the *Zohar*[3] the above Talmudic source is quoted with added detail: When a Jew comes home from *shul* on Friday eve, the

---

3. *Zohar Chadash* 39d.

Shechinah (Divine Presence), with a retinue of angels, accompanies him. Finding the candles burning, the table set, and husband and wife greeting each other affectionately, the *Shechinah* declares: "This is My home — 'Israel,' in whom I take pride!"[4] Finding it otherwise, the *Shechinah* departs, and the angels leave with it. The *Yetzer hara* and his evil hosts take their place, the *Yetzer* declaring: "This is my home; these people are mine!" and a spirit of *tumah* (uncleanness) sets in.

Our Sages observe that a husband and wife — איש and אשה — have the *Shechinah* among them, as represented by the letters *yud* and *hey*, respectively, forming G-d's Name. When the *Shechinah* departs, and the *yud* and *hey* disappear, what is left is אש and אש (*esh* and *esh*), "fire" and "fire."

The keynote of Shabbat — as we had occasion to note — is peace and harmony, joy and holiness.

The *Tikkunei Zohar*[5] points out further, that if a person has a disagreement or quarrel with his wife, or with anyone else, during the week, he should be certain to straighten the matter out before Shabbat, so that he be at peace with everybody when Shabbat comes. And if he has been at peace with everybody during the week, an extra measure of goodwill and love should be shown to one another, reflecting the peace and harmony that reigns On High on this holy day.

Blessing the Children

In many homes it is customary for the father to bless the children on Friday eve, since it is a very auspicious time, as noted above, and the blesser and the blessed are both on a higher spiritual level. According to some authorities there is also a further reason for this custom, namely, that it sometimes

---

4. Isaiah 49:3.
5. *Tikkun* 21.

happens during the week that the father had to use the "rod" to discipline a child, when the child's misbehavior called for a spanking or a harsh word. So now is the time to strengthen their mutual love through a fatherly blessing, to which the angels will also say "*Amen.*"

The way a father blesses his children is the way our father Jacob blessed his grandchildren Efraim and Menasheh. It will be recalled that he put his hands on their heads and blessed them, saying: "By you will Israel bless (their children), saying: 'G-d make you as Efraim and Menasheh.'"[6] Similarly, the father places his hands on his son's head and blesses him, saying: "G-d make you as Efraim and Menasheh."

When blessing a daughter, he says "G-d make you like Sarah, Rivkah, Rachel and Leah." Then, in both cases, he recites the three-fold priestly blessing, "G-d bless you and protect you. G-d make His face to shine upon you and be gracious unto you. G-d lift up His face towards you and grant you peace."[7]

The reason why Jewish boys are blessed that they be like Efraim and Menasheh is that they were truly model children, of whom their father Joseph and grandfather Jacob could be justly proud, certain that they will carry on the great tradition and heritage of the Jewish people. Moreover, they deserved all the greater credit because, even though they were born and raised in Egypt, they were fine and wonderful Jewish children.

As for girls, there could be no better model for them than the mothers of our people, Sarah, Rivkah, Rachel and Leah.

And for Jewish parents and grandparents there is no greater joy than seeing their children and grandchildren, boys and girls, grow up in the way of the Torah, learning Torah and doing Mitzvot and, in due course, seeing them raise their own children in the same way. This is what true *Yiddishe nachas* is all about.

---

6. Genesis 48:20.
7. Numbers 6:24-27.

שלום עליכם

Shalom Aleichem

The hymn *Shalom Aleichem* consists of four stanzas, each of which is repeated three times. It reads:

> *Peace unto you, ministering angels, angels of the Most High, of the King of kings, the Holy One, blessed be He.*

> *You have come in peace, angels of peace, angels of the Most High, of the King of kings, the Holy One, blessed be He.*

> *Bless me with peace, angels of peace, angels of the Most High, of the King of kings, the Holy One, blessed be He.*

> *Depart in peace, angels of peace, angels of the Most High, of the King of kings, the Holy One, blessed be He.*

This beautiful hymn, which is recited or chanted on returning from *shul* on Friday evening, was composed by an unknown poet, most likely a saintly Kabbalist, several hundred years ago. It is not found in the text of earlier *Siddurim*, nor in the *Siddur* of Yemenite Jews. However, the hymn has become part of the Jewish tradition of both Ashkenazi and Sephardi Jews.

The last verse, "Depart in peace...," seems a little strange. Why should we tell the angels to leave? The likely explanation is that since we are about to sit down to eat the first Shabbat meal, and we cannot very well invite the angels to join us, for angels do not eat, we send them off politely and with honor.

After the hymn it is customary to recite two appropriate verses from Tehillim:

> *For He orders His angels to you, to guard you in all your ways.*[8] *G-d will guard your going out and coming in from now and for evermore.*[9]

---

8. Psalms 91:11.
9. Psalms 121:8.

אשת חיל
Eishet Chayil

Next, the beautiful hymn, *Eishet Chayil* (a Woman of Valor) is recited. This alphabetical hymn (each verse beginning with a letter of the *aleph-beit,* from *aleph* to *tav*) is the conclusion of the Book of Proverbs,[10] composed by King Solomon. We shall quote here only the first two and last two verses:

> *A woman of valor who can find? For her price is far above rubies. The heart of her husband trusts in her, and he shall lack no gain.... Grace is false and beauty is vain; but a woman that fears G-d, she shall be praised. Give her of the fruit of her hands, and let her works praise her in the gates.*

On the face of it, it is a glowing tribute to the Jewish wife and mother. It enumerates her many virtues; she does good and no evil all the days of her life; she takes care of her home, husband and children; she is kind to the poor and needy; she speaks with wisdom and loving-kindness and, above all, her greatest virtue is that she is a G-d-fearing woman.

But, in a deeper sense, our Sages say, *Eishet Chayil* is the Torah itself, to which the Jewish people is "married." The Torah is the "wife"; the Jewish people — the "husband." The Jew trusts in the Torah, and the Torah takes care of the Jew. The Torah cannot be estimated in terms of gold and silver and precious stones. It is all virtue and loving-kindness (*"Torat-Chesed"*), and the source of all blessings.

Another allegorical interpretation sees in *Eishet Chayil* an allusion to the Jewish people, in whom "the heart of her husband (HaShem) trusts"; and so forth in this vein.[11]

---

10. Ch. 31:10 ff.
11. *Zohar III*, Leviticus *Tazria* 42b.

סדר קידוש לליל שבת

KIDDUSH FOR SHABBAT

i

The first Shabbat meal, which is on Friday night, begins with
Kiddush, the Prayer of Sanctification. According to Jewish law,
the Mitzvah of *Kiddush* is properly fulfilled only if it is recited at
the place of the *se'udah* (meal).

In some congregations, however, it is customary to make *Kiddush* also in the synagogue, before the end of the Friday night
service.

The custom of making *Kiddush* in the synagogue dates back to
the time of the Talmud. In those days, and for centuries afterwards, the synagogue was the place where wayfarers and the
poor of the town would find free shelter and meals in a side-room attached to the synagogue, which also served as a hostel.
As wine could not be provided for everyone, it was customary
for the *chazzan* to make *Kiddush* for them in the synagogue, at
the conclusion of the Friday night service, so that those eating at
the synagogue hostel could have their meal immediately. Thus,
the above-mentioned law was fulfilled. Later, when meals were
no longer served at the synagogue, there seemed no reason to
continue the custom of reciting the *Kiddush* in the synagogue,
and, indeed, many congregations discontinued the practice.
Other congregations, however, continued the custom for various
reasons. One, that a custom which has become sacred through
the centuries is often maintained even if the original reason for it
no longer existed. Another reason was that it is stated in the
Talmud that the Shabbat *Kiddush* has healing powers. One of
the great authorities, the author of *Or Zarua,*[1] states that the

---

1. Rabbi Isaac of Vienna, 13th century, was a disciple of Rabbi
   Simcha Vitri, a disciple of *Rashi.*

84

main purpose of the public *Kiddush* in the synagogue is simply a proclamation of the holiness of the Shabbat before the gathered congregation. At any rate, whether the custom is maintained or not, both views are based on Jewish Law.

Whatever the reason for *Kiddush* in the synagogue, it is clear that the *Kiddush* commanded in the Torah is the one made at home, immediately before the *se'udah* on Friday night. It is into our homes, more so than in the synagogue, that we must bring the holiness of the Shabbat.

The *Kiddush* is recited on wine, which makes the occasion a festive one, and emphasizes the importance of the *se'udah*; it is not simply a "meal" that we eat on Shabbat but a *se'udah*, a feast, in honor of the Shabbat Queen, a celebration of the great gift which G-d has given us — the holy Shabbat.

In the Ten Commandments, the Torah states: "Remember the Shabbat day to sanctify it."[2] This means — according to the interpretation of the Sages of the Talmud — that we are commanded to sanctify the Shabbat (i.e., pronounce its holiness) by reciting the *Kiddush* over wine, both on Friday night when Shabbat begins, and again during the day (though the text of the *Kiddush* varies for each meal).

A further reason why *Kiddush* is recited over wine is that wine has been endowed by the Creator with a special quality of gladdening the hearts of men.[3] Indeed, when it is used for a holy purpose, it also gladdens G-d, as it is written, "(wine) gladdens G-d and men."[4]

Explaining the significance of wine in connection with Shabbat, the *Zohar* declares that Shabbat is the "bride" of the Jewish people, and just as the betrothal of a bride (called *kiddushin*, "sanctification") is recited over wine, so is *Kiddush* recited over

---

2. Exodus 20:8.
3. Psalms 104:15.
4. Judges 9:13.

wine. This also indicates with what joy the *Kiddush* has to be recited!

The *Zohar* observes that the *Kiddush* on Friday night contains 70 words (in two parts of 35 words each) which relate to the numerical value for the Hebrew word for wine — yayin (יין).[5]

However, if wine is not available, the *Kiddush* may be recited over bread — the two Shabbat loaves, *lechem mishneh*, which, incidentally, also represent husband and wife.

Women, too, are commanded to observe the Mitzvah of *Kiddush*, even though Shabbat and *Kiddush* are connected with a certain time and women are, as a rule, exempt from Mitzvot that must be performed at a specific time. *Kiddush* is an exception to the rule. Our Sages explain this by the fact that the words *zachor* and *shamor*, with which the commandment of Shabbat in the first and second Ten Commandments respectively begin, were pronounced by G-d simultaneously, "in one utterance," as already noted earlier.[6]

This extraordinary miracle (coupled with the miracle of the two words being comprehended distinctly, which normally is humanly impossible) was to underscore the intent of the commandment that insofar as Shabbat is concerned, those obligated to observe the *"don'ts"* (under the heading *shamor*), namely both men and women, are also included equally in the *"do's"* of *zachor*, particularly *Kiddush*.

Thus, while the husband usually recites the *Kiddush* also for the wife, she must intend to be included, and partake of the *Kiddush* wine as well. If the husband is away and no other male of at least Bar-Mitzvah age can do so, she must make *Kiddush* herself.

In the same way as *zachor* and *shamor* were pronounced at the same time, the other variations in the Ten Commandments were also pronounced simultaneously. This explains the differences in

---

5. *Zohar III, Emor* 95a; *Tikkunei Zohar, Tikkun* 23.
6. See p. 29.

the texts of the Shabbat commandment, where, for example, in the first Ten Commandments it is stated that Shabbat is a remembrance of the Creation, while the second Ten Commandments relates it to *yetziat mitzraim*. Both are, of course, true, and go hand in hand together, as the *Ramban* explains.[7]

ii

The first part of *Kiddush* consists of *Vayechulu* — the section from *Bereishit* which speaks of the completion of the Creation of the world by the seventh day, which G-d sanctified, making it a day of rest — the holy Shabbat. This is the origin of Shabbat, and the Torah makes it clear how Shabbat came into being as a Divine creation.

We have already discussed this section of the Torah at some length, since *Vayechulu* is said twice before *Kiddush*, during the *Amidah* of the Friday night prayer and again immediately afterward. The main significance of reciting this portion on Friday night is to give testimony to the fact that G-d is the Creator of the world, and that He ordained the Shabbat as a holy sign and clear evidence of this fact.

The second part of *Kiddush* should be recited with equal joy and inspiration, for it is like the other side of the same coin. Not only does it contain the same number of words, as mentioned above, but it also explains and complements the first part. The blessing over the wine, which is recited between the two sections of *Kiddush*, joins them together.

The second part begins with a blessing and ends with a blessing. It begins with the blessing,

> *Blessed ... Who has sanctified us with His command-*
> *ments.*

This form is familiar to us from the text of other blessings

---

7. See *Ramban* (Nachmamidis) on Deut. 5:15.

which we make when we do Mitzvot. We thank G-d, the Source
of all blessings, for giving us His commandments, since through
His Mitzvot we attach ourselves to G-d and share in His holiness. There is no man-made holiness, and ours is not of our
making. But by bringing holiness into our daily life through the
fulfillment of G-d's Mitzvot, we draw holiness upon ourselves
and are part of our "holy nation."

The *Kiddush* continues:

> ... *and has taken pleasure in us; and with love and plea-
> sure He has given us His holy Shabbat as an (everlast-
> ing) inheritance; a memorial to the work of Creation.*

The words, "(He) has taken pleasure in us" (or "desired us"),
mean that it was G-d's desire and pleasure to choose us for the
purpose of giving us His commandments and bestowing His
holiness on us. This is also why He gave us His holy Shabbat as
an everlasting inheritance. Moreover, He gave us the Shabbat
"*with love and pleasure*"; for although the Shabbat entails many
restrictions, it is a most wonderful gift which G-d gave us
because He loves us. By the same token we accepted the Shabbat
with love and pleasure (for the words can be understood both
ways). Indeed, He gave us the Shabbat even before He gave us
the Torah, for the first laws of Shabbat were given to our people
in Marah (before coming to Sinai) in connection with the wonderful Heavenly food, the manna, which rained down from
Heaven during the forty years in the desert.[8] (The manna first
came down thirty days after the Exodus from Egypt, twenty
days before the giving of the Torah). This is also one of the
reasons why Shabbat is "a remembrance of the going out of
Egypt." Thus the *Kiddush* continues:

> *First of the holy festivals, a remembrance of our going
> forth from Egypt.*

---

8. Exodus 16:11-35.

In the *Sidra* Emor,[9] where all the festivals are enumerated, Shabbat is mentioned first.

The Shabbat reminds us of the Creation as well as of *yetziat mitzraim*, the liberation of our people from Egypt.

To be sure, according to some authorities, such as the *Tur*[10] and *Abudraham*,[11] the words "a remembrance of our going forth from Egypt" refer to the "holy festivals" (Pesach, Shavuot, Succot), which are more directly connected with *yetziat mitzraim*. But this does not rule out the fact that Shabbat itself is also related to it. Indeed, in the second Ten Commandments[12] the Torah mentions it explicitly, and the *Ramban*, in his commentary on that verse, explains this connection.

The point of it is this: the Shabbat reminds us, first of all, that G-d is the Creator of the world. But some people might think that perhaps, after creating the world, G-d left it to take care of itself, and takes no further interest in it. Some people might become so accustomed to nature and the natural order of things as to forget altogether that there is a Creator. Some people might even think that behind every force in nature there is a separate "god": a god of thunder and lightning, a god of fire and a god of water, a god of light and a god of darkness, a god of war and a god of peace, and many other gods that fight each other and create havoc in the world, as the worshippers of idols thought.

The Jewish people, ever since the first Jew Abraham, have always believed in the One G-d, the Creator of heaven and earth, and the Master of the whole world. And it was the Divine intervention leading to *yetziat mitzraim* that convinced them beyond the slightest doubt that what they believed was absolutely true. For our ancestors in Egypt saw with their own eyes the won-

9. Leviticus chap. 23.
10. Par. 271.
11. 52b.
12. Deuteronomy 5:15.

drous miracles — the ten plagues in Egypt and the miracles at the crossing of the sea — and knew that G-d was the Supreme Master of the world and of all the forces of nature, which He can change at will. When, therefore, they later stood at the foot of Mount Sinai and saw the Divine Revelation and heard G-d begin the Ten Commandments with the words, "I am G-d, your G-d, who brought you out of Egypt, from the House of Bondage" — they knew Who was speaking to them. Thus, by keeping the Shabbat we are reminded of the Ten Commandments and of *yetziat mitzraim*, and we give living testimony to the great and eternal truth that G-d is not only the Creator of the world, but also its ever-watchful and all-powerful Master, and He alone rules the world as He sees fit in His infinite wisdom.

This is why the holy Shabbat is a living memorial to both the Creation and *yetziat mitzraim,* as we say in the *Kiddush.*

iii

In conclusion, *Kiddush* reaffirms the chosenness of the Jewish people and its unique destiny, in which Shabbat has a central role:

> *For You have chosen us and sanctified us from among*
> *all peoples, and Your holy Shabbat, with love and favor,*
> *You have given us as an inheritance. Blessed are You,*
> *G-d, Who sanctifies the Shabbat.*

"*You have chosen us.*" Many people, including some Jews, find it difficult to understand why G-d has chosen one people, the Jewish people, and made them holy by giving them the Torah and Mitzvot. Why just one people? Why the Jewish people? Why make it different from all other nations of the world?

G-d is the Creator of the world, and He has His own thoughts and plans as to how to conduct the world He created, and He alone truly knows what is really good for all His creatures. Yet in many cases G-d has revealed some answers in His Torah and through His prophets. Such is the case also in regard to the question of His chosen people. Let us begin with a simple illustration, which will help us understand what being G-d's chosen people means.

A human king rules over all his subjects, but he chooses his personal servants for special duty. He commands all his army, yet he chooses a special regiment, which he calls his "royal regiment." He rules over all his land, and cities, and villages, yet he chooses one city for his personal residence, his royal palace. This does not mean that by choosing his personal servants and royal regiment he takes no further interest in any of his other subjects, or the rest of his army, just as making his residence in a certain city does not mean that he has given up the rest of his country. It does mean, however, that his personal servants have special duties to perform, and being in the very presence of the king, they must always be on their best conduct. Similarly, the members of the royal regiment, who bear the king's insignia, must be model soldiers. Also, the city that is the king's residence must be kept particularly clean and beautiful.

In the Torah which He gave us on Mount Sinai, G-d tells us that He created the world, and that His plan included a chosen people who would be "His people," who would have the special duty to spread G-dliness on this earth. He would give this chosen people His Torah and Mitzvot, both as the guide in their daily life and the source of G-dliness which it was their duty to spread in the world.

The Torah further tells us how this Divine plan began to unfold. Our father Abraham, who, living in a generation of pagans and idol worshipers, was the one and only one to recognize One G-d, the Creator of heaven and earth. And when Abraham chose G-d, G-d chose Abraham and made an everlasting covenant with him, promising him that his descendants would be the chosen people, who would be given the Torah and a land as an everlasting inheritance.

Choosing the Jewish people, the children of our patriarchs Abraham, Isaac and Jacob, was not the only choice G-d made.

Within the Jewish people themselves, G-d chose one tribe, the tribe of Levi, for special service; and within the tribe of Levi, G-d chose one family, that of Aaron, for greater service as *kohanim* (priests), who alone could perform the holy service in the House of G-d, the *Bet Hamikdash*.

Having chosen the Promised Land to be the one land on earth that would be recognized by all the peoples of the world as the Holy Land, "the land which G-d's cares for, and His eyes are continuously upon it, from the beginning of the year to the end of the year,"[13] G-d saw fit to choose within this land one city, the holy city of Jerusalem (also called Zion); and within this city G-d chose one place, Mount Moriah, on which the *Bet Hamikdash* was to be erected. Even within this holy Sanctuary there was a section called the Holy of Holies, where the most chosen one of the people — the *kohen gadol* — was allowed to enter only on the holiest day of the year — Yom Kippur. This was the occasion, once a year, that brought together the three most chosen and holiest dimensions in the world: time, place and person, and it was part, indeed the highlight, of G-d's plan of spreading G-dliness and holiness on this earth, and making this earthly world a fitting "abode" (לעשות לו דירה בתחתונים) for G-d's Presence.[14]

Many are the Biblical passages that speak of G-d's selection of the Jewish people, of Abraham the father of the Jewish nation, of the Land of Israel, of Jerusalem, of the tribe of Levi, of Aaron as father of the *kohanim*. Only a few such passages can be mentioned here:

On the selection of Abraham: "You are the L-rd G-d who have chosen Abram... and made the Covenant with him...."[15]

On the selection of the people Israel: "You are a holy nation unto the L-rd your G-d; the L-rd G-d has chosen you to be His

---

13. Deuteronomy 11:12.
14. *Midrash Tanchuma, Nasso* 16.
15. Nechemiah 9:76.

treasured people from all the nations on the face of the earth...
and you shall keep the commandments, and the statutes and
judgments which I command you this day to do them."[16]

On the selection of Zion and Jeursalem: "For G-d has chosen
Zion..."[17] and "Jerusalem, the city which G-d chose to set His
name on it."[18]

On the selection of the tribe of Levi, and Aaron: "For the L-rd
your G-d has chosen him (Levi) from all your tribes, to stand
and serve in the Name of the L-rd..."[19] and "Aaron, whom He
chose."[20]

On Isreal choosing G-d: "And Yehoshua said to the people:
You are your own witnesses that you have chosen G-d, to serve
Him...."[21]

Clearly, G-d has been quite "selective" in His choices for
creating this world, in the center of which He placed His chosen
people and the Torah.[22]

The duties and privileges that G-d bestowed upon His chosen
people are *spiritual*: they have to do with leading a holy life in
accordance with the Torah and Mitzvot, by which they constantly proclaim and attest to the unity of G-d, the Creator and
Master of the world. This basic principle is clearly stated and
emphasized numerous times in the Torah. It finds expression in
the *Kiddush*: "*For You have chosen us and sanctified us.*" So, also,
in the blessing over the Torah: "*Who has chosen us from all
nations and given us His Torah.*" Likewise in the *Amidah* prayer
of Yom-Tov: "*You have chosen us from all nations... and have
sanctified us with Your commandments.*" This concept of "being

---

16. Deuteronomy 6:6-11.
17. Psalms 132:13.
18. Kings I 14:21.
19. Deuteronomy 18:5.
20. Psalms 105:26.
21. Joshua 24:22.
22. Rashi on Genesis 1:1.

chosen for service and holiness" is reiterated every time the selection of the Jewish people is mentioned in the Torah, and in all of Scripture as well as in our prayers and blessings. G-d has chosen the Jewish people neither because it is the greatest or mightiest of all nations, nor to rule over other nations nor to lead an easy life, but solely to be a "kingdom of *kohanim* (G-d's servants) and a Holy Nation."[23]

That G-d made a good choice is proven by the long history of our people. Though it be a history of persecution, suffering and martyrdom, the Jewish people remained faithful to G-d and to the sacred task which He had given them, not only for their benefit, but also for the benefit of all mankind.

---

23. Exodus 19:6.

שחרית לשבת
SHABBAT MORNING PRAYERS

Introduction

The Morning Prayers on Shabbat (and Yom Tov) are considerably longer than on weekdays, for the simple reason (as the *Levush*[1] observes) that people do not have to go to work on Shabbat and there is no hardship involved in spending a little more time in the synagogue. For this reason, in addition to the fact that the Morning Service on Shabbat includes the reading from the Torah of the entire *Sidra* of the week followed by the *Musaf* ("Additional") Prayer, there are a number of special psalms from *Tehillim* which have been added to the *Pesukei d'Zimra*.[2]

We recite the additional psalms on Shabbat, says the *Abudraham*, to distinguish between Shabbat and the weekdays. For Shabbat is a "sign," G-d says, "between Me and the Jewish people... that in six days G-d created the heavens and the earth, and on the seventh day He ceased from work and rested."[3]

It is quite understandable, of course, that we should distinguish between Shabbat and the weekdays in our prayers, since we make Shabbat distinctive in every other way: in the clothes we wear, the food we eat, in our talking and walking. A deeper reason, however, for the lengthier prayers on Shabbat is given by the holy *Zohar*:

> Shabbat is a holy day, dedicated to the service of G-d with joy. When the holy people, the Jewish people, gather in the *shul* to sing G-d's praises, it brings joy in

---

1. *Orach Chayim*, par. 281.
2. See *My Prayer*, Vol. I. op. cit. p. 117 ff.
3. Exodus 31:17.

the heavens and on the earth, and fills the whole universe with the spirit of holiness.[4]

In other words, our Shabbat prayers have an extraordinary significance, and G-d welcomes them with particular pleasure. It is only right that we should "give G-d some more pleasure" on Shabbat by reciting additional prayers.

In this connection the *Zohar* has some very strong words to say about people who do not appreciate the extraordinary privilege of singing G-d's praises on Shabbat, and whose conduct in *shul* is not in keeping with the holiness of Shabbat, nor with the holiness of the place of worship. Observes the *Zohar*:

> When the holy people gather in *shul* on Shabbat they must give their undivided attention to the prayers and the reading of the Torah, and not talk even about worthy matters. Whoever engages in other matters, not to mention worldly matters, is like one who desecrates the Shabbat and has no share in the holy Jewish people. Two angels are appointed on this day to watch how everyone conducts himself in *shul*, and they place their hands on the person who does not conduct himself properly, saying, "Woe to this one, who has no share in the Holy One, blessed be He."[5]

II

There are twelve additional psalms in the Shabbat Morning Prayers (according to *Nusach Ari*), which are not recited on weekdays, the first of which is Psalm 19: "*The heavens declare the Glory of G-d.*"

According to the *Abudraham*, ten of these psalms allude to the ten sayings ("G-d said, 'Let there be...,'" etc.) by which G-d created the world. Psalm 19 alludes to the first, with which

---

4. *Zohar II, Vayakhel,* p. 205a.
5. Ibid.

heaven and earth came into being. The other nine psalms allude to the other sayings: "Let there be light," "Let there be a firmament," and so forth. Psalm 136 — *"Give praise unto G-d, for He is good, for His kindness endures forever"* — refers to the tenth saying, "Be fruitful and multiply," which calls for the birth of good and righteous people who praise G-d for His kindness. Indeed, it is written, "The world is built through kindness."[6]

When were these additional psalms included in our Shabbat prayers?

According to the *Zohar*,[7] the custom of reciting them is as old as the prayers themselves. It was instituted by the Men of the Great Assembly (*Anshei Knesset Hagedolah*) — the sacred body of prophets and sages who (about 2300 years ago) instituted and arranged our daily prayers and blessings as we know and recite them today.

These additional Shabbat psalms and prayers will presently be discussed individually.

השמים מספרים

Psalm 19: Hashamayim Mesaprim

It has been pointed out that the day of Shabbat is a "memorial to the creation of the universe (זכרון למעשה בראשית)." Jewish observance of the seventh day of the week as the holy day of Shabbat, with complete cessation from work and business and the routine activities of the preceding six days of the week, is living testimony to the fact that G-d created the world in six days and "rested" on the seventh day, which He blessed and sanctified as a holy day.

In light of the above, it is appropriate that the first of the special psalms which have been added in the Morning Prayer of

---

6. Psalms 89:3.
7. *Zohar II*, *Terumah* 137b.

Shabbat should be Psalm 19, which begins (after the introductory verse: "For the Choirmaster; a psalm by David") with the verse:

> *The heavens recount the glory of the Almighty, and the sky proclaims His handiwork.*

As we read through this psalm, we can see that it contains three main themes. The first part of the psalm (verses 2-7) speaks of the Creation: The heavens and the earth, day and night, and the rising sun — each and all proclaim the glory of G-d as it manifests itself in the "natural" order and beauty of the created universe.

The second section (verses 8-11) speaks of the Torah and Mitzvot. They are perfect, soul-restoring. They illuminate the mind with wisdom and fill the heart with joy. They are pure, true, just. More desirable than gold and sweeter than honey.

The third section (verse 12-15) expresses personal reflections of a man who knows his purpose in life — as a servant of G-d, scrupulous in observing G-d's precepts, conscious of inadvertent failings, praying for Divine help to avoid falling into sin. It concludes with the familiar verse (with which every *Amidah* is concluded):

> *May the words of my mouth and the meditation of my heart be acceptable before You, O G-d, my Strength and my Redeemer.*

The connection between the three themes of the psalm — G-d, the Torah and man — will become apparent in the light of the teaching of our Sages, as indicated in the Torah itself. The world was created for the sake of the Torah and for the sake of the people of Israel[8] — who were to receive and observe the Torah and Mitzvot, thus bringing G-dliness down to earth and making the physical and material world a fitting "abode" for the Divine Presence.

---

8. *Rashi* on the first word of the Torah — *Bereishit.*

רננו צדיקים
Psalm 33: Ranenu Tzaddikim

The second of the special psalms that have been added in the Morning Prayer of Shabbat (also of Yom Tov) — according to *Nusach Ari* — is Psalm 33. According to *Nusach Ashkenaz* this psalm is recited later on, before Psalm 92.

There is a continuity between Psalms 19 and 33 in the context of the Shabbat theme, and the concluding verse of the former is a fitting introduction to the opening verse of the latter.

Psalm 19 concludes on the subject of acceptable meditation. Such meditation — on the creation of the universe, on the great Divine gift of the Torah and Mitzvot, and on the purpose of man's life on earth, which are the main topics of Psalm 19 — must inspire overwhelming joy in the hearts of the righteous (*tzaddikim*). Hence, the opening verse of Psalm 33. (The term *"tzaddikim"* also refers to all the Jewish people, as it is written, "And Your people are all righteous (*tzaddikim*)."[9]

Psalm 33 begins as follows:

> *Sing joyously to G-d, you righteous ones;*
> *it is fitting for the upright to offer praise.*
> *Express your thanks to G-d with a harp;*
> *Sing to Him with a ten-stringed lyre.*
> *Sing to Him a new song; play well sounds*
> *of jubilation. (vs. 1-3)*

It is a hymn of praise to G-d, who is just and faithful, who loves righteousness and justice, and whose kindness fills the earth (vs. 4-5). Indeed, the entire Creation is an act of G-d's kindness, since "it is in the nature of the Good to do good."[10] Hence, G-d created the world not for His benefit but for the benefit of the creatures.

---

9. *Isaiah* 60:21.
10. Rabbi Schneur Zalman, *Shaar Hayichud VehaEmunah*, ch. 4. quoting Kabbalah.

The psalm continues:

> *By the word of G-d the heavens were made, and by the breath of His mouth all their hosts. (v. 6)*

This beautiful expression refers to the Ten Sayings with which the Creator created the heavens and the earth and all creatures in them, as we are told in the first chapter of Genesis. At the same time, the metaphor of "the word of G-d" provides an illustration that helps us to understand a profound concept, namely, how the creation of the whole universe has not made any change in the Creator, and He remains exactly the same after Creation as before Creation.

Thus, Rabbi Schneur Zalman, the founder of *Chabad* Chassidic philosophy, explains: A word uttered by a human being does not make any change in the person; indeed, one may utter countless words without being affected by them. So the creation of the universe, which came into being "by the word of G-d," has not changed the Creator in the least.[11]

Contemplating the wonder of Creation makes one realize that the Creator is also the Master of the world and of all the nations of the world. Therefore, whatever the thoughts and schemes the nations may have that are contrary to G-d's will are all made null and void by G-d. All this gives the Psalmist a feeling of delight at being a member of the chosen people, and he exclaims:

> *Happy is the nation whose G-d is the L-rd;*
> *(happy is) the people whom He has chosen as His possession. (v. 12)*

Many people, though they believe there is a G-d who created the world, do not necessarily believe or understand that G-d takes a personal interest in their private affairs, or that He really cares how they live and what they do. Many have a vague idea that G-d does somehow guide the destiny of the world, and of nations, but they do not think that they are individuals impor-

---

11. *Tanya*, ch. 20.

tant enough for G-d to be concerned with their thoughts or deeds. This is not the Jewish belief. Jews believe that G-d watches over the world not only in a general way, but in a particular way (*hashgacha pratit*). This concept is the subject of the next verses:

> *From heaven HaShem looks down; He sees all mankind. From His dwelling place He watches closely* (hishgiach — hence Hashgacha) *all the inhabitants of the world. He that fashions the thoughts of them all, perceives all their actions.* (*vs. 13-15*)

To some people G-d is just an "onlooker," with little or no interest. To others, G-d "watches closely," but still in a general way. Both consider G-d's place in heaven, without interfering in human affairs here on earth. But the Torah view is that He who has fashioned (created) human beings with the ability to think, surely knows their thoughts and their actions. And He watches every individual, be he a king or ordinary individual — with an eye to show His kindness to those who fear Him and look to His kindness. (vs. 16-19)

It is noteworthy that the verse, "*He that fashions the hearts of them all, perceives all their actions*" is the only Biblical quotation cited by the great *Rambam* (Maimonides) in his formulation of the Thirteen Articles of our faith. It is quoted in support of the Tenth Article: "I believe with perfect faith that the Creator, blessed be His Name, knows every deed of men, and all their thoughts, as it is said, *He that fashions the hearts (thoughts) of them all, perceives all their actions.*"

Psalm 33 concludes with an expression of complete trust in G-d:

> *Our soul yearns for G-d; He is our help and our shield. For in Him our heart rejoices, for in His holy Name we put our trust.*
> *May Your kindness, O G-d, be upon us, as we place our hope in You.*

Our Sages (in *Midrash, Zohar*, etc.) declare that Psalm 33 (like many other psalms) alludes also to the World To Come (*Olam Haba*) — "the world that is all Shabbat." The allusion is found in the reference to the "ten-stringed" lyre, or harp, as well as to the "new song." The Talmud[12] quotes a *Baraitha* (Tannaic source):

> Rabbi Yehuda said: The harp used in the Bet Hamikdash had seven strings... the harp that will be used in the days of Mashiach will have eight strings... and in the World To Come — ten strings.

In support of this tradition, the author cites Biblical references, including the "ten-stringed" lyre in Psalm 33.

The significance of the numbers seven, eight and ten in this context is: Seven symbolizes the natural order of this world — since the world was created in seven days; *eight* symbolizes the supernatural order, as it will be in the Messianic era; *ten* — the "perfect number" — symbolizes the World To Come that will be all good and perfect.

It is also significant that Psalm 33 has twenty-two verses, corresponding to the twenty-two letters of the Hebrew alphabet with which the Torah was written, and with which G-d created the world.

Thus, Psalm 33 is a fitting addition to the Morning Prayer of Shabbat. For Shabbat is "a memorial to the work of Creation," and it also gives us a "taste" of the World To Come, which will be a perfect world, a world that is fully at rest and peace under the Kingdom of HaShem.

לדוד בשנותו

Psalm 34: L'David Bshanoto

Psalm 34 was composed by David — as the introductory verse tells us — "when he pretended to be insane before Avimelech."

---

12. *Erachin* 13b. See also Rashi *ad loc.*

The story is told in Samuel I[13]: David, in flight from King Saul who was jealous of David's popularity, especially after he slew the Philistine giant Goliath, was so hardpressed that he sought temporary refuge in the Philistine city of Gat, where King Achish reigned. (All Philistine kings since the days of Abraham, were called *Avimelech* — "father-king" — in addition to their proper name, just as the kings of Egypt were called *Pharaoh* ("Lord of the great house"). David was recognized by some local inhabitants, whom he overheard saying, "This is surely David, of whom they were singing in the streets, 'Saul has slain his thousands, but David his tens of thousands!'" Realizing that his life was in great danger, David pretended to be insane and began acting like a madman. Achish (Avimelech) could not believe that this madman was David, and let him go.

The *Midrash*, referring to this Psalm, tells us that when David was praising the Creator, saying, "How manifold are Your works, O G-d, You have made them all with wisdom,"[14] he wondered why G-d created insanity. David wondered what good evolves for anyone, when a man walks in the street, tears at his clothes, and children run after him and make fun of him. Then G-d said, "A time will come when you will need it and will pray for it!" The time was not late in coming, when David fled from Saul to Achish, king of Gat. It seemed like yesterday when David slew Goliath, and now he came to Achish with Goliath's sword at his side. Goliath's brother was Achish's bodyguard. When he heard that David was in Gat, he asked the king's help to apprehend him, so that he could avenge his brother's death. But Achish replied: "Your brother was slain in battle, after David accepted his challenge to a duel!"

While this went on David began to fear for his life, and he prayed to G-d, "Master of the World, answer me...."

"What is your wish?" G-d asked.

---

13. Ch. 21:11-16.
14. Psalms 104:24.

"Give me some of that madness which You created...."

David began to act like a raving lunatic. He also scribbled on the gates of the city, "Achish king of Gat owes me one hundred ten-thousands (shekels), and his wife fifty ten-thousands!"

It so happened that the king's wife and daughter were stricken with a bout of madness that day. They were raving inside the palace, while David was raving outside. Impatiently, Achish called to his servants, "Am I short of crazy people that you have brought this one, too? Send him away!"[15]

David was happy that he had been saved through "insanity," and he composed this psalm in alphabetical prose, beginning the first verse with an *aleph*, saying: *I bless G-d at all times; His praise is always in my mouth.* The repetition, "at all times" and "always" is meant to indicate that a person should praise Hashem both in times of well-being as well as in times of distress.

For if a human being cannot see the good that comes in a bitter pill, G-d knows it. And so we find in the account of Creation: "And G-d saw *all* that He created and, behold, it was very good."[16]

David does not stop at praising G-d himself. Feeling gratified in doing so, he wants the humble to hear it and rejoice with him (vs. 1-2). Indeed, he calls upon them: "Exalt G-d with me, and let us extoll His name together" (v. 4). This latter verse is familiar to us, as we hear it from the *chazzan* in *shul* when the scroll of the Torah is taken out of the Ark for the Torah reading.

This verse is also the source of the Rabbinic rule that three or more men who have eaten bread together must say Grace in unison, whereby one invites the other two to join in praising G-d "of whose bounty we have eaten and by whose goodness we live."[17]

---

15. Samuel I 21:16.
16. Genesis 1:31.
17. *Berachot* 45a.

Of the highlights of this psalm we will mention some of the more familiar verses:

Taste and see that G-d is good; happy is the man that trusts in Him.

King David tells us here that our relationship with G-d is something that has to be *tasted*, that is to say, *experienced*, in order to be appreciated. As with delicious food, one cannot know what it tastes like by reading about it or hearing it described; one must taste it. So too is the personal experience of closeness to G-d. It is the actual observance of His precepts in everyday life that provides the taste and real feeling of G-dliness in one's life. This is particularly true of Shabbat and *Yom Tov,* which can be appreciated only through their actual observance in the fullest measure. This is also emphasized in the *Musaf Amidah* of Shabbat — "Those who *taste* it, merit (eternal) life."

Psalm 34 continues:

Come children, listen to me; I will teach you the fear of G-d. Who is the man who desires life, who loves long life to see goodness? Guard your tongue from evil, and your lips from speaking deceitfully. Turn away from evil and do good, seek peace and pursue it.

King David urges us to listen to his fatherly advice and teaching. In several sentences and in carefully chosen words, David gives us the meaning of fear of G-d and the secret of a long and good life. Fear of G-d has to express itself primarily in terms of respect for one's fellow-man, the first requirement of which is to guard one's tongue from speaking evil (*lashon hara*) and deceptions, so as not to hurt anyone, nor one's own self. This is not all that difficult, since a person should be able to control his tongue or, at least, keep his lips sealed if he has nothing good to say.

The Talmud tells us the story of a Sage, Rabbi Alexandri, who came to a city and went into the marketplace, calling out, "Who wants life? I have a prescription for long life!" He was quickly surrounded by many people, clamoring, "Give it to me!" Then the Sage produced a Book of Psalms and read from it: "*Who is the man who desires life, who loves long life to see goodness? Guard your tongue from evil, and your lips from speaking deceitfully!*"[18]

The next step has to do with *action*: "*Turn away from evil and do good.*" Here again it should not be too difficult for a person to avoid doing anything that is wrong in the eyes of G-d — if he has fear of G-d in his heart, and to do only that which is good and right. It is easy to understand that, since G-d is the Creator of man and He expects a person to turn away from evil and to do good, He has surely provided him with the necessary capacity to act and conduct his life in full accord with G-d's Will.

Finally, King David urges everyone to make a special effort to foster peace and harmony in one's own life and in one's relations with others: "*seek peace*" — in your immediate surroundings, "*and pursue it*" — wherever you can.

Our Sages never tired of emphasizing the vital importance of peace as G-d's greatest blessing, which is so much dependent on human effort. "*The Holy One, blessed be He, has found no better vessel to contain blessing than peace.*"[19]

תפלה למשה
Psalm 90: Tefilah L'Mosheh

Psalm 90, beginning with the words, "A prayer by Mosheh, Man of G-d," is the first of 11 psalms (90 to 100) which, according to tradition, were composed by Mosheh Rabbeinu.[20] King David incorporated them in his Book of Psalms along with a number of other psalms composed by various authors (including

---

18. *Avodah Zarah* 19b.
19. End of *Oktzin* and conclusion of the Talmud.
20. See *Rashi* on this verse.

his son Shlomo, Asaph, Heyman, Eitan (Abraham), the Sons of Korah, and others).

The designation "Man of G-d" in the beginning of the psalm suggests that Mosheh did not insert this description of himself, but King David did to identify and describe the author.

The main theme of this psalm is *teshuvah* — generally translated by the word "repentance," but literally meaning "return."

The connection between *teshuvah* and Shabbat — which is one of the reasons why this psalm has been included in the Shabbat morning prayers — will be better understood when we take a closer look into the concept of *teshuvah*.

The central importance of *teshuvah* can be seen from the fact that it runs through the entire *T'NaCh*. Our Sages of the Talmud and *Midrash* have further emphasized the importance of *teshuvah*. One example is the declaration that *teshuvah* is one of the seven things that preceded the creation of the world.[21] In support of this declaration the Sages cite our present psalm:

> *Before the mountains were born, when You created the earth and the world, and for ever and ever You are Almighty G-d; You return (תשב) man to the point of crushing humility, and You say, 'Return, children of man.'*[22]

By saying that *teshuvah* preceded the world, our Sages declare that *teshuvah* is one of the very foundations upon which the world rests.

Why is *teshuvah* so important? First we must see what *teshuvah* is.

Actually there are two kinds of *tehuvah:* a "lower" *teshuvah* and "higher" *teshuvah*.

The first is the kind of *teshuvah* reserved for a sinner: one who actually committed a transgression or failed to do a Mitzvah. *Teshuvah* opens the way to a complete Divine pardon. If G-d

---

21. *Midrash Tehillim* on Psalms 90, par. 12.
22. Psalms 90:2-3.

had not "created" *teshuvah*, there would be no way and no hope to rectify a wrongdoing and obtain a complete pardon from G-d. Man would then sink ever deeper in the quagmire of sin, and the world would become devoid of G-dliness — a dismal place indeed for mankind. But G-d desired the world to be an "abode" (*ma'on*) for His Divine Presence in every generation (v. 1). Therefore, before He created the world He created *teshuvah*, giving every person the ability and encouragement to return to G-d. Indeed, a heavenly voice continuously calls out: "*Return, children of man!*" Thus, everyone is assured that sincere *teshuvah* is graciously accepted by G-d, and the slate will be wiped clean to start a new life at any time a person resolves to do so.

Furthermore, G-d has set apart certain times and periods in the year which are marked by particular Divine grace and mercy to accept "returnees." Best known and most favorable is the period of the Ten Days of *Teshuvah*, from *Rosh Hashanah* through Yom Kippur, at the beginning of every year.

It is, of course, preferable that a person do *teshuvah* on his own free will. But if, despite all the encouragement and opportunities to do *teshuvah*, a person fails to respond, G-d may find it necessary to bring a man "to the point of crushing humility" to impel him to return. Then he calls out to G-d "out of the depths,"[23] and G-d answers him.

The second kind of *teshuvah* — the "higher" *teshuvah* — is not associated with sin, be it a sin of commission or of omission. It has to do with a constant striving to get ever closer to G-d through ever greater excellence in serving Him in every aspect of everyday life. It also has to do with the natural development of a person as one grows older and wiser from day to day. This is the kind of *teshuvah* that pertains to the sinless and saintly men who spend every waking moment in Torah study, prayer and good deeds. Yet, as a day passes, and the *tzaddik* reviews his progress

---

23. Psalms 130:1.

along the never-ending road of goodness and holiness leading ever closer to G-d, he feels a deep sense of failure that his standards and goals of yesterday were not higher in light of his knowledge today. This feeling of *teshuvah* is heightened when the Ten Days of *Teshuvah* come around — even if the *tzaddik* has not knowingly committed a single transgression. For him the thought that he could and should have done better is sufficient to evoke the deepest yearning for *teshuvah* and the most determined resolve to do better henceforth.

It is this "higher" form of *teshuvah* that is more closely associated with Shabbat. Both have the identical purpose: to raise the individual to a higher spiritual level and bring him closer to G-d. What *teshuvah* does for a person, whatever his spiritual level, Shabbat does as well. However satisfactory the past six days may have been in terms of Divine service, on the holy Shabbat a Jew is elevated to a higher spiritual level. Observed properly, Shabbat brings the experience of a return to the source, namely, the return of the Divine soul — which since its descent into this material world must inevitably be involved with material things — to its source in Heaven. For when Shabbat comes and the Jew puts out of mind all cares and distractions of the six *working* days, his Divine soul is released from its material shackles, able to freely "return" home for a whole day (twenty-six hours,[24] the numerical equivalent of the four-lettered Divine Name). The Shabbat experience then serves as a spiritual stimulant for the weekdays ahead.

The identity of purpose common to both Shabbat and *teshuvah* is indicated also in their very names, since they comprise the identical Hebrew letters (though in a different order): תשב-שבת.[25]

---

24. Although a day has only 24 hours, extra time is added to Shabbat by ushering it in before sunset and terminating it well into the night.

25. Rabbi Schneur Zalman, *Tanya Iggeret HaTeshuvah*, ch. 10; *Likkutei Torah, Devarim* 66:3.

יושב בסתר
Psalm 91: Yoshev B'Seter

He that dwells in the shelter of the Most High, abides in the shadow of the Almighty (v. 1).

The *Midrash*[26] declares that Mosheh recited this psalm when he went up to Mount Sinai and "dwelt in the shelter of the Most High." The *Midrash* further points out that there is an allusion to the 120 days and nights that Mosheh spent on Mount Sinai (three times did he ascend forty days and nights) in the word בצל ("shadow") in the second part of the first verse. The two letters צ"ל equal 120. Thus, in the first verse of the psalm, Mosheh Rabbenu refers to himself.

According to other Midrashic sources,[27] the verse refers to HaShem. It is a salutation to Him who dwells in the hidden place of the Most High, yet He desires to "lodge" in the shadow of the Sanctuary which Betzalel (בצלא-ל) constructed. In other words, HaShem who dwells on High in total mystery, unknown even to angels, prefers to cause His *Shechinah* (Divine Presence) to dwell in a small place on earth, namely in the Sanctuary, from which His light radiates throughout the world. For it is only here on earth that humans have the opportunity and privilege to worship Him with heart and soul, study His Torah and carry out His Mitzvot with self-sacrifice and dedication.

Rashi, in his usual way of explaining the basic meaning of the text, interprets the first verse as follows: The person who takes shelter in the Most High — who puts his complete trust in G-d — will certainly find himself secure and safe under the "shadow" (protection) of HaShem. Thus Mosheh Rabbenu opens his psalm by urging everyone to put one's complete trust in G-d.

---

26. *Tanchuma, Nasso.*
27. *Midrash Rabbah, Shemot* ch. 34; *Bamidbar,* ch. 12.

According to several commentators,[28] the entire psalm is dedicated to such times and occasions when the Jewish people as a whole, and Jews individually, find themselves in Exile *(Galut)* or in any kind of distress. At such times, in particular, Jews must put their trust in G-d, pray to Him and rely on His help with complete confidence.

The special connection with Shabbat is found in the following verse:

> *For He will instruct His angels in your behalf, to protect you in all your ways.*

Here is an allusion to the two angels accompanying a Jew on Friday night on his way from *shul*, mentioned earlier.[29]

The *MaHaRShA* explains that every Mitzvah (not only Shabbat) has two appointed angels, one from the Right (the side of holiness) and one from the Left (the "other side"). The first is to testify in favor of a Jew performing the Mitzvah; the other is to testify against the one who fails to perform the Mitzvah. In the end both must testify in favor, or against as the case may be, to confirm the testimony (since the Torah requires *two* witnesses).

According to the *Zohar*,[30] the two angels mentioned in the verse also refer to the *yetzer tov* (good inclination) and *yetzer hara* (bad inclination). The *yetzer hara* comes to a person from the moment of birth, as it is written, "At the threshold (of life) sin lurks."[31] It continuously tempts a person to seek the pleasures of the body. On the other hand, the *yetzer tov* comes to a person only at the age of Bar Mitzvah (and Bat Mitzvah) — in order to help the person oppose the *yetzer hara* and to encourage him (and her) to carry out the Mitzvot which they must now fufill as full-fledged adult Jews. When a person follows the encouragement of the *yetzer tov* and overcomes whatever temp-

---

28. *Me'iri*, Ibn Yachya, *Sforno*, and others.
29. See p. 78.
30. *Zohar* part I, *Vayyishlach* 165b.
31. Genesis 4:7.

tation or obstacle is in the way, the subdued *yetzer hara* is forced to answer "*amen*" and becomes a partner in the performance of the Mitzvah, since now it can be carried out wholeheartedly and with joy. These are the two angels that accompany all persons everywhere to protect them in all their ways.

Psalms 98; 121-124

The following five psalms (according to *Nusach Ari*), namely, Psalms 98, 121-124, followed by Psalm 135, bring to ten the number of psalms added to the Shabbat Morning Prayer. The number is significant, for it corresponds to the "Ten Divine Fiats" by which the world was created.[32] This is a further allusion to one of the fundamental aspects of Shabbat as a "memorial to the work of Creation."

Since we have already discussed Psalm 98 as it appears in *Kabbalat* Shabbat, we will proceed with Psalm 121.

אשא עיני אל ההרים
Psalm 121: Esa Einai

A Song of Ascents. I lift my eyes to the mountains — from where will my help come? My help will come from the L-rd, Maker of heaven and earth. He will not let your foot falter; your guardian does not slumber. Indeed, the Guardian of Israel neither slumbers nor sleeps. The L-rd is your guardian; the L-rd is your (protective) shade at your right hand. By day the sun will not harm you, nor the moon at night. The L-rd will guard you from all evil; He will guard your soul. The L-rd will guard your going and your coming from now and for all time.

---

32. *Avot* 5:1.

The main theme of this beautiful psalm is, obviously, G-d's benevolent providence.

Sometimes, on the brink of despair, a person may wonder, "From where will my help come?" But the person who believes in G-d will immediately feel reassured for, however "hopeless" the situation may seem, surely there isn't anything that G-d cannot do; nothing is impossible for the Creator of heaven and earth! Indeed, the psalmist assures the person who trusts in G-d that G-d will not let him down.

The Jewish people, dispersed as a small minority among the nations of the world, have often had difficult times; it almost seemed as if G-d was "asleep," and didn't know, or didn't care, what was happening. But, of course, Jews always knew, and took heart in the fact, that the Guardian of Israel neither slumbers nor sleeps.

Our Sages commented on the somewhat unusual expression, "I lift my eyes to the mountains." They saw in the word הרים ("mountains") an allusion to the word הורים ("ancestors"). Thus they read in the first verse of this psalm, "I lift up my eyes to the *patriarchs*." We Jews often recall the memory of our patriarchs, Abraham, Isaac and Jacob, and their complete dedication to G-d. Not only are we inspired by their deep trust in G-d, but we also appeal to G-d to be gracious to us for their sake.

It has also been noted that there is a special connection between "mountains" and our patriarchs. A mountain may not seem so very tall from a distance, but the closer you get to it, the taller it gets. So too with our patriarchs and, indeed, with all our great men and women: the more you learn about them, the more you appreciate their greatness and saintliness.

The example by which the psalmist compares G-d's protection to the "shade" also has a deeper meaning. The Hebrew word צל "shade," also means "shadow." Hence, the Baal Shem Tov taught, "Hashem is your shade" also means "HaShem is your *shadow*." A person's shadow does exactly what the person does. If the person moves quickly, so does his shadow; if he lifts his hand, so does his shadow, and so on. This is also the meaning of the words, "HaShem is your shadow": when you reach out to another person who is in need and help him, G-d does the same for you; when you bring joy to another person, G-d fills your heart with joy; when you bless another person, G-d Himself blesses you, and so on. In other words, G-d rewards *in kind*, but in a very generous measure.[33]

The notion of G-d's "guardianship" (as in the words *guardian* and *guard*) is mentioned six times in this short psalm. This underlines that G-d's protection is needed each and every day of the week, while the holy seventh day, Shabbat, is in itself especially blessed with G-d's protection and peace.

שמחתי
Psalm 122: Samachti

Psalm 122 is a beautiful hymn dedicated to the holy city of *Yerushalayim,* the city of "awe" (*yirah*) and "peace" (*shalom*). It was composed by David in a spirit of prophecy, seeing a vision of the city and the *Bet Hamikdash* crowded with the joyous pilgrims coming from all the tribes of Israel.

The opening verse of this psalm reads:

> *A Song of Ascents by David. I was rejoiced when they said to me, "Let us go to the House of the L-rd."*

Our Sages observed that David was referring to unsavory individuals who gathered under his windows and called out tauntingly, "Let's go to the House of the L-rd...." They knew how much David wanted to build the *Bet Hamikdash*, but HaShem had reserved this great privilege for his son Shlomo. However, far from being pained by these calls, David said,

---

33. See also Rabbi Schneur Zalman *Torah Or, Miketz* 36c; *Likkutei Torah, Balak* 74c.

"Though I know that these people expect me to be vexed, I am joyous to note their eagerness and impatience to see the *Bet Hamikdash* built."[34]

Our feet stood firmly within your gates, O Jerusalem!

Here, according to the interpretation of the Talmudic sage Rabbi Yehoshua ben Levi,[35] King David expressed his acknowledgement that the reason he and his men were successful in defending the Jewish people against their surrounding enemies ("our feet stood firmly") was due to the "gates" of Jerusalem, meaning the place where the Torah scholars gathered to study and expound the Torah. In other words, in the merit of the Yeshivah students studying Torah, the defending forces were successful in the battlefield.

Jerusalem that is built like a city which is united together.

Our Sages mention several reasons why Jerusalem is called the "City of Unity." According to Rabbi Yochanan, it refers to the idea that the physical city of Jerusalem here on earth has its spiritual counterpart — Jerusalem in heaven, and is the gateway to it, for through the Jerusalem below, all prayers from anywhere in the world ascend to G-d. Indeed, declares Rabbi Yochanan, "The Holy One, blessed be He, says, 'I will not enter the Jerusalem in heaven before I enter the Jerusalem that is on earth.'"[36]

This corresponds to the idea often expressed by our Sages that G-d prefers the praises of His children on earth to those of His angels in heaven, and that the angels are not permitted to sing G-d's praises before the Jewish people have said their daily prayers.

Rabbi Yehoshua ben Levi explains this verse to mean that

34. *Yalkut Shimoni* on this verse.
35. *Makkot* 10a.
36. *Yalkut* on this verse.

Jerusalem unites all the Jews to be real *chaverim*, worthy friends,[37] as mentioned clearly in the following verse:

> *For there the tribes went up, the tribes of G-d — a testimony to Israel — to offer praise to the Name of the L-rd.*

When the Jews of all the tribes of Israel came to Jerusalem on their three annual pilgrimages, they were so awed and inspired by the holiness of the *Bet Hamikdash*, where the Divine Presence was so much in evidence, that they were all permeated with the spirit of fear and love of G-d. Thus they were all united and unified, and G-d Himself could testify to the purity and holiness of the Jewish people.

Moreover, Jerusalem has a central place in the world as a model of justice and morality:

> *For there stood the seats of justice, the thrones of the House of David.*

The psalmist concludes with the following moving lines:

> *Pray for the peace of Jerusalem; may those who love you have peace. May there be peace within your walls, serenity within your mansions. For the sake of my brethren and friends, I ask for peace within you. For the sake of the house of the L-rd our G-d, I seek your well-being.*

The relevance of this psalm to Shabbat is this: What Jerusalem is in terms of holiness and peace in *space*, Shabbat is in terms of holiness and peace in *time*. And both, rooted in G-d's Torah and Mitzvot, are the eternal bonds that unite and unify all Jews, all the Jewish people.

---

37. In Talmudic times, חבר was a title of distinction applied to especially observant, scholarly Jews. In later times the title was used in some communities in a symbolic way.

אליך נשאתי

Psalm 123: Elecha Nassati

A Song of Ascents. To You have I lifted up my eyes, You who dwell in Heaven. As the eyes of servants are turned to the hand of their masters, as the eyes of a maid to the hand of her mistress, so are our eyes turned to the L-rd our G-d, until He will be gracious to us. Be gracious to us, L-rd, be gracious to us, for we have had more than enough contempt. Our soul has been overfilled with the derision of the self-satisfied; with the scorn of the arrogant.

According to our Sages, "lifting up one's eyes to Heaven" is more than a gesture of prayer. It means that one should see, that is, understand, that the cause of everything is in Heaven. In other words, whatever happens here on earth is no accident, but something that has been ordained in Heaven by Divine providence. Therefore, if something unpleasant happens to a person, it should be taken as an indication that something in his/her behavior has to be rectified.

This verse brings to mind the story of the brazen serpent.[38] When the children of Israel, wandering through the desert, complained that they were fed up with the manna and spoke against G-d and against Mosheh, they were punished by an attack of poisonous snakes that bit and killed many of them. Our Sages explain that it was a fitting punishment, since an evil tongue is like the fangs of a snake, which kills without deriving any benefit for itself. Realizing their sin, the children of Israel repented and begged Mosheh to pray for them. This he did immediately and G-d told him to make a snake of brass and set it upon a high pole, so that any one bitten by a snake could look up and live. Observed our Sages, "Did the brazen serpent possess the power to kill or bring back to life? Of course not, but so long as Jews

---

38. Numbers 21:4-10.

lifted up their eyes and subjected their hearts to their Father in Heaven, they were saved."[39]

As the eyes of servants turned toward their masters.

There are times when we pray to G-d, "Have mercy on us like a father who is merciful to his children." And sometimes (as in this psalm) we compare ourselves to servants or slaves. (In the days of slavery, a slave was totally at the mercy of his master).

There are two principal ways of serving G-d. One is inspired by fear (awe) of G-d, the other by love of G-d. The first is likened to the service of a servant, and the other to the service of a son. Each has its advantage and disadvantage. A servant serves his master with greater humility and will always be careful not to arouse his master's displeasure; he may only do his duty, and no more. A son will readily give his life for his father, and will not consider it a "duty" but a pleasure and privilege to do the things his father asks. On the other hand, because of his familiarity and love for his father, which he knows is mutual, he may sometimes lack the sense of humility and obedience that the servant has. This is why we are expected to serve G-d both as a servant and son combined, that is to say, with the humility and obedience of a servant (or slave) combined with the love and devotion of a son. This is also why we sometimes address G-d as our King or L-rd, and sometimes as our Father in Heaven. If we wish to emphasize our complete dependence on G-d and our utmost humility, we speak of ourselves as G-d's "servants" and slaves; if we wish to express our love and devotion, we speak in terms of a father-son relationship.

It is interesting to note that, commenting on Genesis 32:6, where Jacob tells Esau: "I have oxen, and donkeys, and sheep, and men-servants and maid-servants," the *Midrash*[40] declares that our Patriarch Jacob was alluding to the qualities of his

39. *Rosh Hashanah* 29a.
40. *Bereishit Rabbah* 75:7, 12.

children, the Jewish people, in their service to G-d; their service is with the strength of an ox, the endurance of a donkey, the submissiveness of a sheep, and the obedience of a servant and maid. In this connection the *Midrash* quotes the verse in Psalm 123:2:

> *Be gracious to us, L-rd, be gracious to us...*

In our holy tongue, the word חן (grace), from which the Hebrew verb meaning "to be gracious" is derived, signifies the quality of being kind to someone even where one hasn't done anything to merit any favor. Thus, when we appeal to G-d to "be gracious to us," we are, in effect, saying, "We know that You (our King and L-rd) do not owe us anything, since there is nothing we could possibly do *for You*; nevertheless, we pray *be gracious* to us, for we have already endured more than enough contempt and scorn from our enemies, who are enjoying tranquility and prosperity, yet persecute us for no other reason except that we are Your servants."

לולי השם
Psalm 124: Lulei Hashem

Psalm 124 continues the theme of Psalm 123, namely, our dependence on G-d at all times, especially in times of trouble. It begins as follows:

> *A Song of Ascents by David. Were it not for the L-rd who was with us — let Israel declare — were it not for the L-rd who was with us when men rose up against us,* then they would have swallowed us alive in their burning rage against us.

It has been noted before that King David expressed in the Psalms not only his own feelings, but also those of our people Israel. Thus, when he says in the opening verse, "let Israel declare," he refers to the Jewish people.

In the *Midrash*, however, the opinion is expressed that
"Israel" here refers to our patriarch Israel (Jacob), and that it
was he who recited this psalm as well as all the 15 "Psalms of
Ascent" (*Shir Hama'alot* — Psalms 120-134) during the 20 difficult years he spent in Laban's house.[41]

> *Then the waters would have flooded us, the torrent
> would have swept over our soul; then the raging waters
> would have swept over our soul.*

"Water," especially "raging water," is often used as a metaphor for a flood of troubles that sometimes befall a person at
once. If they came one at a time, it would be easier to cope with
them; but if they all happen at the same time it would be impossible to cope with them — were it not for G-d's help.

The repetitious phrases — "the waters would have flooded
us" and "the torrent would have swept over our soul" — though
not unusual in poetic Biblical style, may also refer to two types
of danger: physical and spiritual. The Jewish people as a whole
and Jews as individuals, dispersed among the nations of the
world and as a tiny minority in most places, have often faced
both types of danger: physical attacks, pogroms and massacres,
as well as religious persecution, efforts by missionaries and various cults to convert Jews, influences of the environment, assimi-
lation, and similar forces. As a result, Jews have always faced
the ever-present danger of being "swallowed up" by the nations
of the world. Were it not for G-d's intervention, the proverbial
"single sheep among seventy wolves" could not have survived
very long.

The metaphor is meaningful also in another sense. A river,
flowing peacefully, may suddenly turn into a raging torrent, due
to a heavy rainfall or melting snow and ice. Or a tidal wave,
caused by a distant earthquake, may suddenly overwhelm peaceful shores and sweep away everything in its path. Something like

41. *Bereishit Rabbah* 68:14; 74:8. *Yalkut* and *Shochar Tov* on this
    verse.

this happened often in Jewish history: for years a Jewish community would flourish peacefully, contributing richly to the development of the country or city in which it flourished. Then, for one reason or another, mainly envy and hatred, the people would turn against their peaceful, defenseless Jewish neighbors like a raging, merciless flood, ready to "swallow them alive" — and would have surely done so were it not for G-d's mercy.

This is why we say, with King David,

> *Blessed is the L-rd who did not let us become prey for their teeth.*

Even in a most critical situation, where a Jewish community or Jewish family seems hopelessly trapped, help comes in a miraculous way:

> *Our soul escaped like a bird from a fowler's snare; the snare broke and we escaped. Our help is in the Name of the L-rd, the Maker of heaven and earth.*

הללוי׳ הללו
Psalm 135: Haleluyah Halelu

Psalm 135 is a hymn of praise to HaShem. It begins with a call:

> *Praise the L-rd. Praise the Name of the L-rd; offer praise,*
> *O servants of the L-rd...*

The plain sense of the words is clear: We call upon each other, especially upon the devoted servants of G-d, to praise Him because He is good and sweet, and because He has chosen us as His beloved treasure (vs. 3-4).

But the Hebrew text of the opening verse lends itself also to another interpretation: "Praise the Name of the L-rd; praise the servants of the L-rd" (i.e., praise both Hashem and His servants). The meaning can be explained by means of the following parable:

A blind man who had to travel to another country obtained a visa to enter that country. Now, the blind man could not travel on his own, so he took with him his companion who served as his "eyes." When they came to the border crossing, the blind man was permitted to enter but his companion, who had no visa, was not. Said the blind man: "Without my companion, my seeing eyes, I am lost. You have to let him through, too!"

Something like this happens in our relationship to G-d. We are required to fear G-d, love Him, praise Him and, most importantly, follow in His ways. But many people do not know, nor have they learned, how to do this. Therefore the Torah teaches us that the commandment to fear and love G-d includes also to respect and love G-d's servants, the Torah scholars and *Tzaddikim* who devote all their time and dedicate their lives to the study of G-d's Torah, and serve Him with all their hearts. For by observing these servants of HaShem and seeing how they conduct themselves in their everyday life, we can follow their example. Without them — without our spiritual leaders, Rebbes and teachers — we would be like the blind man who had to go into a strange country needing "seeing eyes" to lead him.[42]

> *Praise the L-rd, for the L-rd is good: sing to His Name, for He is sweet.*

Not everything that is good and useful is necessarily sweet and pleasant; just as not everything that is sweet is necessarily good and useful. But G-d is both good and sweet, even though His goodness sometimes comes down disguised in unpleasant wrappings. But that in itself is also for a good purpose, and only G-d knows what is truly good for a particular person at a particular time. That is why we must always thank G-d and praise Him, in good times as well as in bad. For what appears to us as "bad" is

---

42. *Yalkut* on this verse.

undoubtedly a blessing in disguise. For inasmuch as G-d is good, and it is in the nature of the good to do good, nothing bad could come from Him.

> *For G-d has chosen Jacob for Himself, Israel for His beloved treasure.*

The construction of this verse in Hebrew is such that it can be understood also the other way: "For Jacob has chosen G-d for himself; Israel (has chosen G-d) for his beloved treasure." Both versions are true. It was Abraham, the first Jew and father of our people, who first discovered G-d and dedicated himself to spreading the knowledge of G-d on earth, whereupon G-d chose him to become the father of G-d's Chosen People, the people of Israel (Jacob).

Among the praises of G-d that this psalm mentions are that He is the Creator of heaven and earth, creating everything He desired in the heaven and on earth, in the seas and in all depths; that He is the Maker of rain, raising mists from the earth to return in the form of rain, accompanied by lightning and winds.

Further on there is a reference to the miracles of *Yetziat Mitzraim*, the liberation of the Jewish people from Egypt. This was an act that equalled Creation itself, for it clearly demonstrated that G-d was indeed the Creator and Master of the world, who could change the laws of nature at will.

The Creation of the world and *Yetziat Mitzraim* are topics that are directly connected with Shabbat, which, as we have mentioned, is a "memorial" to both.

Next there is a reference to the Land of Israel, on both sides of the Jordan River (the lands of Sihon and Og on the East Bank, and the lands of the Canaanites on the West Bank), which G-d gave to our people as an everlasting inheritance.

Finally there is a reference to the Day of Judgment, when G-d will show compassion for the Jewish people, "His servants," and will recompense them for all their suffering during their dispersion among the nations of the world. Then all those who had trusted in man-made idols, idols deaf and dumb and sightless, will become like them — meaning that they will acknowledge their failings and seek new vision and new teachings and a new life in the knowledge of G-d that will fill the earth. That will be the time when every Jew — *Kohen*, *Levi* or Israelite — will join with all who fear HaShem, and proclaim (in the words of the concluding verse):

> *Blessed is the L-rd from Zion, who dwells in Jerusalem. Praise the Lord.*

הודו להשם

Psalm 136: Hodu L'Hashem

Psalm 136 comprises twenty-six verses of praise to G-d, each concluding with the refrain, *for His kindness is everlasting*. The number of verses corresponds to the numerical equivalent of the Divine Name (*Yud* - 10; *Hay* - 5; *Vav* - 6; *Hay* - 5 = 26). This is one of the reasons why this psalm is called *Hallel Hagadol* (the "Great Hallel") — a play on the words *gadol* ("great") and *umehulal* ("praiseworthy") in the verse, "Great is HaShem and exceedingly praiseworthy."[43]

Our Sages explain that the 26 verses of praise to G-d are significant also in that they allude to the 26 generations of the human race that preceded the giving of the Torah at Sinai. Since the world was created for the sake of the Torah (as *Rashi* comments on the *first* verse of Genesis), and without Torah it could not exist on its own merits, the world was sustained during this period entirely by G-d's boundless kindness.[44]

The 26 generations (2448 years) comprise the ten generations from Adam to Noah; another ten from Noah to Abraham; and the next six generations, namely, Isaac, Jacob, Levi, Kehat, Amram and Mosheh.

---

43. Psalms 145:3.
44. *Pesachim* 118a.

Psalm 136 is very close in content to Psalm 135, with particular emphasis on the Creation of the world and on the miraculous liberation of the Jewish people from Egyptian slavery. These are the two highlights of Shabbat as a "memorial to the Creation" and as a "memorial to the Exodus from Egypt," as noted above.

The 26 Divine acts of kindness enumerated in this psalm are expressed in a few, clear words. Some of these expressions are particularly significant because of their deeper meaning, as noted by our Sages. For example:

Praise Him Who alone performs great wonders. (v. 4)

These words refer to the first wonders that G-d performed when He created the world — the heavens, the earth, the sun, the moon and the stars (as enumerated in the subsequent verses). However, there is also a hidden meaning to this verse, which was revealed to us by our Sages. Sometimes, G-d performs wonders *alone* without showing them to us; only He knows of them, while we remain unaware. The Sages cite an example of two merchants who planned to board a ship. One of them got a splinter in his foot, missed the boat and was terribly upset. What he did not know was that what happened to him was a miracle because the ship went down at sea. Therefore a person should always thank G-d for whatever happens to him, even if it seems not so "good," because it is one of these hidden wonders known only to G-d, saving him from more serious harm.[45]

Praise G-d who struck Egypt through its first-born.

Our Sages[46] tell us that this refers not only to the tenth plague that finally forced Pharaoh to let the Jewish people go from his land, but also to the punishment the Egyptians received in this connection at the hand of their own first-born, even before the plague. For when they heard of Mosheh's warning that unless the Jews were freed, all the first-born would die, they organized

---

45. *Niddah* 31a.
46. *Midrash Tehillim* on this verse.

a huge demonstration in front of Pharaoh's palace demanding
that the Jews be allowed to go. Pharaoh sent out his soldiers to
quell the rebellion. In the bloody battles that followed, tens of
thousands of Egyptians died. This took place on the tenth day of
Nissan, when, according to Mosheh's instruction, every Jewish
household set aside a lamb for the *Pesach* sacrifice four days
later, on the fourteenth of Nissan. The tenth of Nissan before the
Exodus was Shabbat, and that was when the first-born Egyptians learned what was in store for them and rose in rebellion.
The miracle that happened that day gave it the name *Shabbat
HaGadol*, the "Great Shabbat."

Further on, Psalm 136 refers to the miraculous crossing of
Yam Suf (the Reed Sea), G-d's wonders in leading His people
through the desert, and giving the Promised Land to the People
of Israel as an everlasting heritage. Finally there is also an allusion to the future redemption of our Jewish people, and the
ultimate recognition of HaShem by "all flesh" — all mankind —
who will join in praising G-d in Heaven for His everlasting
kindness.

האדרת והאמונה
Ha'aderet VehaEmunah

In *Nusach Ari*, Psalm 136 is followed by the hymn *Ha'aderet
vehaEmunah*. In other *Nuschaot*, this hymn is known from its
inclusion in the *piyutim* of the Morning Service on Yom Kippur.

The source of this hymn is in *Pirkei Hechalot*,[47] a mystical
Midrash said to have been taught by Rabbi Yishmael ben Elisha
Kohen Gadol, one of the ten martyrs who were cruelly executed
by the Romans in the period from the destruction of the *Bet
Hamikdash* through the religious persecution of the reign of
Emperor Hadrian.

47. *Perek* 26, Mishnah 7.

The hymn is composed in double alphabetical order, each verse consisting of two Divine attributes beginning with the same Hebrew letter, and ending with the refrain *L'Chai Olamim*, "to Him who lives forever," the Eternal.

Thus the first verse reads, *Ha'aderet veha'Emunah* (Power and Trust) — *l'Chai Olamim*. The second verse, *HaBinah vehaBra-chah* (Understanding and Blessing) — *l'Chai Olamim*, and so on.

According to the above-mentioned *Midrash*, this hymn is recited by the angels in heaven singing the praises of G-d. In light of this, the *MaHaRIL* and other commentators and author-ities emphasize that this hymn is to be recited in the synagogue with great reverence and solemn melody.

The general meaning of this hymn is that all the attributes that can be enumerated are true and perfect only when applied to G-d, who is eternal and absolutely perfect. But when they are applied to a mortal human being, they cannot be true, because a human being has a limited life on earth and all his qualities are necessarily limited and imperfect. Thus the power of a human king or ruler is only temporary; the trustworthiness of a person is unreliable; a person's circumstance might change, his under-standing is limited, his knowledge incomplete.

Besides, the average person is unlikely to have *all* good and desirable qualities, though he may have a few of them. In any case, he must be careful to use his good qualities in the proper channels and in the right direction.

All this should cause every person to feel very humble, indeed — certainly when he stands before G-d.

It should also be understood that when it is said, "Power and trust — to the Eternal," it means that power and trust *belong* to G-d; they are His. In other words, G-d is the *source* of power and of trust, understanding and blessing, etc. It is not we who bestow these qualities on Him, but the other way around; because He is the source of all good qualities, he bestows some measure of these qualities on us in order that we make good use of them, and this means using them in accordance with His instruction.

Commentators on our prayers and sacred hymns point out that the praises offered by man in *Ha'aderet vehaEmunah* begin with the attributes of power and trustworthiness because they allude to the first praises the Creator received from the water and heavens, two of His earliest creations. Thus it is written, "More than the sounds (literally, "voices") of many waters, the mighty waves of the sea, the L-rd is mighty On High."[48] In other words, the mighty waters of the sea seem to raise their voices in praise and acknowledgement of HaShem, who is truly the Mighty One (*adir*, from the same root as *aderet*).

At the same time, the heavens join in praising the Creator's trustworthiness, as it is written, "You established Your trustworthiness (*emunatecha*) in the very heavens."[49] In other words, the permanent and unchangeable nature of the heavens proclaim the everlasting trustworthiness and faithfulness of their Creator.

נשמת כל חי
Nishmat Kol Chai

The prayer *Nishmat kol chai* ("The breath of all living") is a hymn of praise to G-d, and its main theme is the miracle of the liberation from Egypt. That is why it is said immediately after the "Song of Moses," which Moses and the children of Israel sang after the crossing of the Reed Sea. That is also why our Sages sometimes call this prayer *Birchat Hashir* (the Blessing of the Song).

The prayer *Nishmat* is said during the Morning Prayer on Shabbat and on Festivals, but not during the weekdays. *Nishmat*

48. Psalms 93:5.
49. Psalms 89:3.

is one of the special additions to the Shabbat and Festival prayers, because on the Shabbat and Yom Tov we abstain from work and have more time to recite longer prayers.

For the above reason *Nishmat* is recited also on the first two nights of Pesach (the *Seder* nights), since it so relevant to the festival of our freedom from Egypt.

Nishmat is one of the oldest of our prayers. It is mentioned in the Talmud and various Sages are named as its author. Some say it was the famous sage, Rabbi Shimon ben Shatach, brother of Queen Shelomit (wife of the Hasmonean king Alexander Yannai); his name may be found backwards using first letters of certain phrases: *Shochen ad, Mi yidmeh, Ad heina, Ve-ilu phinu, Nishmat* — forming the Hebrew word *Shimon*. In a similar way the name of Yehoshua ben Nun is found in the prayer of *Aleinu*, which is thought to have been composed by him.[1]

This beautiful and inspiring prayer begins by declaring that the "breath of all living" and the "spirit of all flesh" bless and praise the Name of the L-rd our G-d, the only G-d and the everlasting G-d.

Aside from You, we have no King and Savior...

We continue. We have no one to turn to in times of distress, except G-d, for

He redeems and saves and sustains and answers and has mercy, in every time of distress and tribulation (tzarah v'tzukah).

These various expressions of G-d's help are used not just for style. G-d's help comes in different ways. Sometimes, when Jews are threatened, G-d punishes and destroys their enemies, as they are also the enemies of G-d and of all mankind. At other times G-d brings about a change of heart in these wicked people. The Egyptians and Pharaoh are an example of the first kind of deliverance, when G-d showed "His mighty arm"; the story of Purim

---

1. See *My Prayer*, Vol. I, p. 240.

is an illustration of the way G-d brought about a change of heart in King Ahasuerus, who himself ordered the hanging of Haman.

Similarly there are different kinds of troubles that face our people: sometimes it is a *tzarah* (a threatened calamity) that everyone can see; sometimes it is a *metzukah*, an inner plight not always apparent to all, yet more dangerous. In every case, G-d

> *who leads His world with kindness and His creatures with mercy...*

takes care of us. G-d is infinitely kind, and it is in His very nature to do good. He even has mercy on those who deserve stern judgment. If indeed, our fate were always entirely decided by our own virtues and merits, who could be sure of his future? But we do not claim to be so righteous; we rely, rather, on G-d's mercy and kindness. And as long as we *try* to live according to His Will, we can be quite confident of G-d's help, no matter how great the trouble seems to be. Sometimes, as mentioned above, we may not even be aware of any threat. G-d, however, knows, for He watches over every one of us.

> *For, behold, G-d slumbers not, nor sleeps....*

Of course, G-d does not sleep a wink, so what is meant here is that G-d never for a moment even turns His attention away from everything that is going on in the world; G-d is ever watchful, and nothing big or small, open or secret, escapes His attention.

That is why we want to thank G-d constantly for the great favors that He bestows upon us. But we can never praise and thank G-d enough.

> *Even if our mouth were full of song as the sea, and our tongue full of exultation as the multitude of its waves, and our lips full of praise as the expanse of heaven, and our eyes shine like the sun and the moon, and our hands spread out like the eagles of the sky, and our legs as fleet as the deer...for the myriads of times You have done favors, miracles and wonders for us and for our forefathers of old.*

Many we can enumerate: G-d freed us from Egypt, fed us manna when we were hungry, saved us from the sword of Amalek, Antiochus, Haman, etc.; He constantly saves us from disease and all kinds of suffering and pain. We pray, therefore, that, as

> *until now Your mercies helped us, and Your kindnesses did not leave us, forsake us not, O L-rd, our G-d, ever.*

This prayer should not be said in a hurry; we ought to think deeply about G-d's kindness to us, and how we owe everything to Him. If we would but realize this, we would never stop singing G-d's praises, not only with our soul and breath, but with every part and limb of our body.

> *For unto You every mouth shall give thanks, and unto You every tongue shall swear allegiance, and unto You shall every eye look, and unto You shall every knee bend, and before You shall every figure bow down; and all hearts shall fear You... as it is written, 'All my bones shall declare: O G-d, who is like unto You!'*

This is the reason why we sway while reciting our prayers. How can we stay still when not only our soul but our whole body wants to join in praising G-d? Just as every fiber of our Divine soul seeks expression, through prayer, to be united with G-d, so every limb and organ of our body wants to be absorbed in G-d. This is what is called "ecstasy." Not everyone can reach an "ecstatic state"; too many people read the familiar prayers either too quickly, or without real concentration, often without even hearing properly what they are saying. It becomes too much of a habit. Yet familiarity need not necessarily make it so. People eat three times a day, and usually *enjoy* every meal. We pray three times a day, and if we would but give our prayers a little more thought, we would find great inspiration and uplift in them. At least, on the holy day of Shabbat and on the most happy days of the festivals, we should pray with greater devotion.

The first thing that is essential is at least to know the meaning and translation of the words of the prayers. If we cannot concentrate *every* day on the *entire* prayers, it would be a good idea one day to concentrate on one part, the next day on the next part, so that in the course of a week we will have concentrated on all the prayers. Certain prayers, however, particularly *Shema* and *Shemone Esrei*, must always be said with special concentration and devotion.

Let's learn to pray! This, basically, is the message of *Nishmat Kol Chai.*

הכל יודוך
Hakol Yoducha

That G-d is the Creator of the world is something we must remember every day, and constantly bear in mind. It is only then that we can truly declare that G-d is One, as we say in the *Shema*, morning and evening. That is why the *Shema* is introduced by two prayers (blessings).

The first of these, *Yotzer or* ("the Creator of Light"), speaks of G-d's wonderful creation, which *"in His goodness He renews every day, constantly."* Because of its importance (particularly as a memorial to the creation of the world), Shabbat prayers include additional praises and prayers on this subject.

The opening blessing of *Yotzer:*

> *Blessed . . . Who creates light and creates darkness, Who makes peace and creates all things.*

This blessing is the same on Shabbat as on weekdays. But instead of continuing with *hameir laaretz* ("Who gives light to the earth"), as we say on weekdays, we begin with *hakol yoducha* ("All shall praise You"). It is the first of three special prayers which we say before we return to the regular daily prayer. The other two are: *Keil Adon* ("G-d is Master over all creatures") and *Lakeil asher shavat* ("Unto G-d Who rested on the seventh day").

Hakol Yoducha begins with a declaration that all created

things praise G-d. Not only man, but everything that G-d created is evidence of G-d's greatness and holiness. G-d is "holy" in the sense that He is beyond our understanding; for He is the Creator of everything, men and angels alike, and no created being, not even an angel, can understand G-d.

From praising G-d we now thank G-d for the kindness and mercy with which He daily, constantly, takes care of the whole universe. Every morning G-d "*opens the gates of the East and the windows of the sky*," sending out the sun to give light and warmth to the world and its creatures. The sun is never late, never too hot or too cold for the creatures to bear; every night He sends out the moon to brighten the dark sky. Every minute of the day or night, we can see G-d's goodness, great care and endless wisdom with which He watches over the world. From His works, we can perceive that there is a great King and Master of the world, but He is too exalted and too holy for us to understand. To the Creator of the world and merciful King we address our petition for mercy and for our very existence and life.

We conclude this section of the prayer by saying that there is none to equal G-d, nor is there anything except G-d. By this we mean that in spite of the great wonderful world we live in, with the majestic sun and other heavenly bodies, there is nothing that has any semblance to or comparison with the Creator Himself. Moreover, since everything depends upon the Creator for its very existence and life, and He (as stated earlier in this prayer) "in His goodness renews every day, constantly the work of Creation," there is, in the final analysis, nothing but the Creator Himself. Finally, we mention the four worlds that span our destiny: this world that we live in; the "next" world, after life on this earth (a purely spiritual world of the souls); the period when *Mashiach* will come, when our people will be restored to its former glory in the Holy Land; and finally the time when the dead will be resurrected and this world will attain its highest perfection. We have four worlds but One G-d, Who does not change and who reigns supreme from the beginning of days to the end of days.

א-ל אדון
Keil Adon

Keil Adon is a prayer-poem written in alphabetical order (each verse beginning with a letter in the order of the Hebrew *aleph-bet*). It is a hymn of praise to G-d, the Master of all creatures, and it was composed alphabetically to illustrate that the world was created by the *word* of G-d and for the sake of the Torah, written in the twenty-two letters of the Hebrew alphabet.

The first stanza speaks of the Creation as a whole and of G-d's majesty and goodness which fills the world. The second stanza speaks of the Heavenly Throne and the Divine majesty among the angels. The rest speaks of G-d's great wisdom in creating the heavenly bodies, especially the sun and the moon with their great power and influence upon the earth, and how they too fulfill the will of their Creator with joy and with awe.

It is interesting to note that the first two verses have five words each, a total of ten words corresponding to the ten commands with which the world was created. The next eighteen verses have four words each, totalling seventy-two, corresponding to the highest numerical combination of the Divine Name. The last two verses have six words each, totalling twelve, corresponding to the number of constellations, which is quite appropriate, as they speak of the "heavenly host," that is, the stars.

לאל אשר שבת
LaKeil Asher Shavat

This prayer, which is the third addition to the prayer of *Yotzer* on Shabbat, is a direct continuation of the previous prayer, the last verse of which reads:

All the hosts on high give praise unto Him...

Then follows the hymn which begins with the words:

To G-d who rested from all His works...

Thus, this hymn is a prayer of praise to G-d who created the Shabbat as a rest day.

Let us read on:

On the seventh day He ascended and sat upon His Throne of Glory; He robed Himself in beauty for the day of rest, and called the Shabbat day a 'delight.'*

Having created the world, including man, in the six days of Creation, G-d was exalted and He ascended and sat upon His throne. Before the Creation, there was no one to call Him king, and no one for whom to sit on the throne. But now G-d was truly the King, with the whole Creation, and especially man, to acknowledge His Divine majesty. For this occasion G-d robed Himself in beauty. "Beauty" (in Hebrew, *tiferet*) is the quality of justice tempered with mercy. This is the Divine "robe," for He rules the world with justice, mingled with mercy. Were He to rule the world with stern justice alone, it would be difficult for any creature to justify its existence, and hence the world could not exist. In His kindness, G-d tempered stern justice with mercy, so that the sinner will not be immediately destroyed, but have a chance to better himself, and G-d will forgive him. This is

---

* The second part of this passage, "*He robed Himself in beauty for the day of rest*," has also been rendered: *He garbed the day of rest with beauty* (*Siddur Tehilat Hashem*, translated by Rabbi Nissen Mangel, and in other Siddurim). I prefer the former rendition because, in almost all instances where the verb עטה appears in T'NaCh, it is used (in *Kal*) in the sense of *to wrap (or cover) oneself with*. With על (but not with -ל, as here ליום) it indicates *to put a covering upon* (Lev. 13:45), or *to cover one with* (Psalms 89:46). In the latter two instances the *Hiph'il* form is used.

a Divine quality that we must imitate. There is yet another thing
which we should imitate. G-d "robed" Himself in honor of the
Shabbat to show us how to honor this holy day of rest. We, too,
put on our special Shabbat clothes in honor of the Shabbat, and
we call the Shabbat a "delight" by making everything delightful
for this day, including special Shabbat dishes.

> *This is the praise of the Shabbat day — that G-d rested
> on it from all His work.*

The essence of the Shabbat, its real purpose and its true
praise, is that on it G-d rested from His work. Obviously, this is
not meant to convey that G-d was not tired and needed a rest, as
the word "rest" is understood in relation to a human being.
What it means is that after everything was created in the Six
Days of Creation, G-d *ceased* — did not create anything new —
in the Seventh Day and made this day holy. When He later
commanded us to remember the Seventh Day to keep in holy,
calling it the Day of Shabbat (literally, "Day of Cessation"), He
defined it for us in similar terms. Stated more simply: When
Shabbat arrives, we must consider all activities in which we were
involved during the six work days of the week — finished and
done with; there must be a complete cessation from any further
such activity (comprising all of the thirty-nine kinds of prohibited מלאכות, with all their ramifications, as defined by Hala-
chah). This leaves us free to dedicate ourselves to the holiness of
Shabbat *completely* — physically, mentally, and emotionally,
enabling us to come closest to G-d through the Shabbat
experience.

> *And the Seventh day* [itself] *offers praise and proclaims*:
> '*A Psalm, a Song of the Shabbat day: It is good to give
> thanks unto G-d.*'[1]

The Midrash has something very interesting to say about

---

1. Psalms 92:1-2.

these last words: When Adam, the first man, realized how wonderful the Shabbat was, and how it could bring him closer to His Maker, he prepared to say a hymn of praise to the Shabbat. Said the Shabbat to Adam: "Why should you want to sing a hymn in *my* honor? Let us better both join in singing praise to G-d, for it is good to give thanks unto G-d."[2]

By this beautiful allegory, our Sages teach us that when we honor the Shabbat we honor G-d. For in so doing, we acknowledge, and declare our allegiance to His Majesty, the King of the world, the Creator, who on this day "sits on His Throne, robed in beauty."

And so we read on:

> *Therefore let all His creatures glorify and bless G-d; give praise, honor and majesty to G-d, who is King and Creator of all things, for, in His holiness, He gives an inheritance of rest to His people Israel on the holy Shabbat day.*

We conclude this hymn on the theme of light, with which we begin the blessing of *Yotzer*:

> *For the excellence of Your handiwork, and for the bright luminaries which You have made, they will glorify You forever.*

*   *   *

The prayers from here until the *Amidah* are the same as during the weekdays, and were explained in the first volume of this series.

---

2. *Midrash Tehillim, ad loc.*

תפלת שחרית לשבת

THE SHABBAT MORNING AMIDAH

The *Amidah* of the Shabbat morning service stands mainly under the sign of *Mattan Torah,* the giving of the Torah at Mount Sinai. Thus the theme of *Yetziat Mitzraim* is really continued, since the purpose of the deliverance from Egypt was to receive the Torah. But there is also a direct connection between Shabbat and *Mattan Torah,* for it was early on a Shabbat morning (on the 6th of Sivan, in the year 2448 after Creation) that the entire Jewish people stood at the foot of Mount Sinai and watched with awe the revelation of the Divine Glory on the mountain, and heard with a trembling heart the Ten Commandments.[1]

Instead of a quote in the *Amidah* from the Ten Commandments to "Remember the Shabbat day to keep it holy,"[2] the section *V'Shamru* is quoted, in which G-d declares the Shabbat as a sign of His covenant with the Jewish people, as will be discussed later.

Sometimes the Shabbat itself is called the "Bride," and the Jewish people, the "Bridegroom," as we already know from the special hymn *Lecha Dodi.* In this context, Mosheh Rabbenu is the happy "Matchmaker" who brought about this union. This goes back to the time when the children of Israel were still in Egypt. Our Sages[3] tell us that when Mosheh was still young and a favorite of king Pharaoh, he went out to see his enslaved brethren. Moshe was quite heartbroken when he found that they were made to work hard day after day without rest. He went before the king and told him: "O, Great King! A master who

---

1. Exodus 20.
2. Ibid., 20:6.
3. *Shemot Rabbah* 28.

138

owns slaves does not work his slaves to death, but gives them a
day of rest so that they could go on working for him for a long
time. If you will not give your Hebrew slaves one day of rest,
they will soon die from overwork. But give them one day of rest,
and they will be able to work much better every day." Pharaoh
agreed, and Mosheh arranged that his brethren should rest on
the day of Shabbat. One can imagine how happy Mosheh was
when, later, G-d delivered His people, brought them to Mount
Sinai, gave them the Torah, and made Shabbat observance one
of the Ten Commandments.

If the deliverance from Egypt was the "engagement" between
the Bride and Bridegroom, *Mattan Torah* was the "marriage"
and consummation, and the Torah is the "covenant" or "marriage contract" attesting to the everlasting union between G-d
and the Jewish people. Thus, G-d, the people of Israel and the
Torah are inseparable. The Shabbat is the holy day when this
union came to be. Every Shabbat, therefore, highlights the most
important event in the world — *Mattan Torah.*

ישמח משה
Yismach Mosheh

The above is the basis of the prayer *Yismach Mosheh* (Mosheh
rejoices), with which the central blessing of the Shabbat morning
Amidah begins. The text of it reads:

> *Mosheh rejoices in the gift of his portion,*
> *For You called him a "faithful servant."*
> *A crown of glory You placed on his head*
> *When he stood before You upon Mount Sinai,*
> *And he brought down in his hand two tablets of stone*
> *On which was inscribed the observance of Shabbat.*
> *And thus it is written in Your Torah...*

"*Mosheh rejoices in his portion.*" The Shabbat was especially
"*his*" portion," for he introduced it to the Jewish people while

still in Egypt, and it was on Shabbat that Mosheh brought down
the tablets with the Ten Commandments.

With all his wisdom and saintliness, with all his great accom-
plishments in leading the Jewish people out of Egypt and receiving the Torah for them, Mosheh was the most humble of men.
His greatest reward was to be called by G-d, "My faithful servant."[4] Any other man might have taken a great deal of credit
for what he had accomplished, and might have been filled with
pride and conceit. But not Mosheh; G-d could trust him.

Our Sages in the *Midrash*[5] tell us the following parable:

A rich man had a choice piece of land and entrusted it to one
of his servants. Said the friends of the rich man to him: "You
might yet lose your field, for now you let that servant eat the
fruit of the field, and soon he will claim that the field is his." But
the rich man answered smilingly: "Any other person might have
been tempted to do so, but not that faithful servant of mine, for I
can trust him with anything that I possess." Thus, our Sages say,
G-d entrusted to Mosheh all the wisdom possible for man to
know, and gave the Torah through him, and even called it the
"Torah of My servant Mosheh"[6] and "the Torah of Mosheh."[7]
But Mosheh claimed no single law, not even the Shabbat, as the
fruit of his own wisdom. That is why G-d rewarded him with a
"crown of glory" which later also shone from his face.

Mosheh "brought down" the tablets of stone; he had "to
fight" for the Torah with the angels, and he *brought it* down to
the level of every Jew, so that every one could study it and
observe its Mitzvot.

"*And thus it is written in the Torah,*" introduces the well-
known Biblical passage *Veshamru*:

And the children of Israel shall observe the Shabbat, to

---

4. Numbers 12:7.
5. *Yalkut* on Numbers 12:7.
6. *Malachi* 3:22.
7. Joshua 8:31 and elsewhere.

*make the Shabbat throughout their generations as an
everlasting covenant. Between Me and between the
children of Israel it (the Shabbat) is an everlasting sign:
that in six days G-d made the heaven and the earth, and
on the seventh day He ceased and rested.*[8]

This famous section from the Torah, like *Vayechulu* and the
fourth of the Ten Commandments, is one of the well-known
passages of the Torah about the Shabbat.

*Veshamru — they shall observe the Shabbat... to make the
Shabbat —* covers the "don'ts" and the "do's" of Shabbat:

The first aspect of Shabbat observance is *not to do* any of the
39 categories of work (with their offshoots) that would *desecrate*
(make unholy) the Shabbat. But that is not enough; we must *do*
many things to *consecrate* (make holy) the Shabbat. These
include — in addition to the pre-Shabbat preparations — such
specific Mitzvot as lighting the candles before sunset, reciting the
Shabbat prayers, making *Kiddush*, eating festive meals, devoting
extra time to Torah study, etc.

"Throughout their generations" — means that the Shabbat
must be kept at *all times*, and in *all places*; there is no exception
whether we are in the desert, in our Holy Land, or in America,
and we must keep it today as did our ancestors a thousand years
ago. We are also obligated to see to it that our children and
children's children will keep it to the end of days.

We must make the Shabbat an *everlasting covenant.* The word
for covenant is *Brit,* and it reminds us of the Covenant of our
father Abraham, circumcision. Just as circumcision is the covenant between our people and G-d, so is the Shabbat another sign
of the same covenant. The first is sealed in our body, and the
second is sealed in our soul; no Jew is complete when one or the
other is missing.

The Shabbat is, further, a *sign,* a mark of distinction, which
makes us G-d's witnesses that G-d is the Creator of the world:

8. Exodus 31:16-17. See also pp. 3 and 7, above.

that G-d created the world in six days, but stopped on the seventh and "rested," in order to make the Shabbat a day of complete work-stoppage, a holy day for the soul (*vayinafash*, "and he rested," comes from the word *nefesh*, soul).

For not only did G-d stop work on this day, He also "made it holy." G-d, for His part, made the Shabbat holy, and we, for our part, must keep it holy. The Shabbat is like a treasure "locked" by two keys, one held by G-d and the other by us, both of which are necessary to open the treasure. Just before Shabbat both "keys" are handed to us and the treasure is ours.

ולא נתתו

V'lo Netato

The section *V'lo netato* is a continuation of the previous theme:

> *And You, O G-d, have not given it to the nations of the lands, nor have You given it as an inheritance to the worshippers of idols; and also in its rest the uncircumcized shall not share. For unto Your people Israel have You given it with love, to the seed of Jacob, whom You have chosen.*

The Shabbat is exclusively Jewish; no other nation in the world has a share in it, for it is the symbol of the loving relationship that exists between G-d and Israel: G-d chose Israel and Israel chose G-d.

In ancient days, heathen nations, such as the Greeks and Romans, scoffed at Jews for "wasting" a whole day each week doing no gainful work. Eventually the Christians and Moslems adopted a sabbath — Sunday for the former, Friday for the latter. But there is no resemblance between the sabbaths of the non-Jewish world and the Jewish Shabbat.

The following sections — *Yismchu*, *Elokeinu* and *Retze*, concluding the central blessing of the *Amidah* — are the same as in the Friday night *Amidah*, except for a change in the conclusion of *Yismchu*, omitting the words "a memorial to His work of Creation." All this is discussed in the section on the Friday night *Amidah*.

* * *

Following the Amidah we recite the "Song of the day."[9] The "Song of the day" for Shabbat is Psalm 92, which was explained with the prayers of Friday night.[10] In some congregations the Song of the Day is recited at the end of the service.

אתה הראת
Atah Horeita

Following the Song of the Day, several selected verses are recited by way of introduction to the order of the Torah reading. These are (in Nusach Ari):

You have been shown to know that the L-rd is G-d; there is none else aside from Him.[11] This declaration was made by Mosheh in reference to the experience of the wonderful Exodus from Egypt, as well as to that of the Revelation and the Giving of the Torah at Mount Sinai.

Your Kingship is kingship over all worlds, and Your dominion is throughout all generations.[12]

The L-rd is King, the L-rd was King, the L-rd will be King forever and ever.[13]

The L-rd will give strength to His people; the L-rd will bless His people with peace.[14] The significance of this verse was discussed earlier.[15]

---

9. See *My Prayer*, Vol. I, p. 205.
10. See pp. 46f.
11. Deut. 4:35.
12. Psalms 145:13.
13. Ibid. 10:16; Exodus 15:18.
14. Psalms 29:11.
15. See p. 25.

סדר קריאת התורה
READING FROM THE TORAH

The custom of reading sections from the Torah in the Congregation on special days dates back to Mosheh Rabbeinu. Thus we find that Mosheh assembled all the people and read to them sections from the Torah pertaining to Shabbat[1] and the Festivals.[2] However, it was Ezra the Scribe who instituted and formalized the Torah readings also on Mondays and Thursdays and other special days. Monday and Thursday were "market" days, when villagers came to town and had the opportunity to attend congregational services. Reading the Torah on Monday and Thursday also makes certain that no three days would pass without Torah reading.

The Torah readings are as follows:

On Shabbat the weekly Sidra is read (beginning with *Bereishit*, on the first Shabbat after Simchat Torah, and concluding with the Sidra *Brachah*, on Simchat Torah. Thus, the entire Torah [the Five Books] is read in the course of the year). Seven male worshippers are "called up" to have a portion of the Sidra read to each. An eighth person is called up for *Maftir* and *Haftarah* (a chapter from the Prophets).

At Minchah on Shabbat, the first part of next week's Sidra is read. Three persons are called up.

On Monday and Thursday, the same first part of the current Sidra is read. Three persons are called up.

Three persons are called up also on each day of Chanukah and on Purim, as well as on Tisha b'Av and other Fast Days (excepting Yom Kippur). The portions read are appropriate to

---

1. Exodus 31:12-17; 35:1-3.
2. Leviticus 1-44. See also Rambam *Hilchot Tefillah*, 12:1.

the occasion. On Thisha b'Av and other Fast Days, the Torah is read also at Minchah, and the third person reads the *Haftarah*. On Tisha b'Av a special *Haftarah* is also read in the morning (by the third person).

On Rosh Chodesh and Chol HaMo'ed (in view of the additional Amida, *Musaf*) four persons are called up for the reading of the designated Torah portions.

On the major festivals five persons are called up, with a sixth for *Maftir* and *Haftarah*.

On Yom Kippur six persons are called up, with a seventh for *Maftir* and *Haftarah*. (When Yom Kippur, or any major festival, occurs on Shabbat, seven persons are called up instead of six and five respectively).

The reading of the Torah is most important, for the Torah is the holiest thing that we possess; it is the wisdom of G-d, and it contains the commandments that G-d has given us and desires us to observe and fulfill in our everyday life. Every time we take out the scroll of the Torah from the Ark, we are reminded of that great event when the Torah was first given to us by G-d on Mount Sinai. All the people stood and trembled in the presence of G-d. It would be too much to expect of us to feel *exactly* the same way every time we see the Torah taken from the Ark, but at least something of those exciting feelings that our ancestors felt on that occasion should enter our heart and mind when the same Torah is taken out to be read to us. And so we stand up the moment the Ark is opened and say a short prayer which is a quotation from the Torah itself.

> When the Torah is taken out, all the people have to come to attention with awe and trembling, and attune their hearts as if they are at that moment standing at Mount Sinai to receive the Torah.[3]

---

3. *Zohar II*, Vayakhel, p. 206a (411).

ויהי בנסוע הארון

Vayehi Binso'a Ha'Aron

When the Ark is opened to take out a Sefer Torah, the following prayer is said:

> *And it came to pass, when the Ark moved forward, that Mosheh said, 'Arise, O G-d, and Your enemies shall be scattered, and they that hate You shall flee before You.'*[1] *For out of Zion shall go forth the Torah, and the word of G-d from Jerusalem.*[2] *Blessed be He who gave the Torah to His people Israel with His holiness.*

During the forty years' wandering through the desert, the Ark with the two Tablets on which the Ten Commandments were written was in the very center of the camp, both when at rest and on the move. Over the *Mishkan* (Sanctuary) hovered a heavenly cloud, and when it rose, it was the signal for the people to move on.[3] The Ark was borne by the men from the tribe of Levi who were especially selected for this task. It was then that Mosheh exclaimed, "Rise up, O G-d, and Your enemies shall be scattered," etc.

The holy Ark leveled a path for the children of Israel, a smooth and safe path. Wild beasts and poisonous snakes all fled before the Ark, and no enemy threatened the Jews on their peaceful march through the desert.[4]

Later also, in times of war, the Ark was sometimes taken and borne into battle, and the enemies of Israel fled before it in terror. As long as the Jews lived with the Torah and followed the Torah, there was no enemy that could harm them. For the enemies of the Jewish people were the enemies of G-d ("Your enemies"), and the enemies of G-d cannot last very long.

And so when we take out the Torah from the Ark in the

---

1. Numbers 10:35.
2. Isaiah 2:3.
3. Numbers 9:15 ff.
4. *Yalkut*, on Numbers 10:35.

synagogue, we remember that solemn exclamation of Mosheh, and repeat it; we, too, pray to G-d to rise and scatter His enemies, the enemies of our people and of our Torah.

We remember also the words of the Prophet Isaiah in his famous prophecy about "The End of Days," when the House of G-d will once again stand in all its glory in Jerusalem, and all the peoples of the world will say:

> Come let us go up to the Mountain of G-d, to the House
> of the G-d of Jacob; and He shall teach us of His ways,
> and we shall walk in His paths; for out of Zion shall go
> forth the Torah, and the word of G-d from Jerusalem.[5]

This is the wonderful picture that presents itself before our eyes when we open the Ark and take out the Torah: that wonderful time, the time of *Mashiach*, when all the peoples of the world will recognize the G-d of the children of Israel as the true G-d, and the Torah His true word and command.

In the meantime, though our people have suffered much (and still suffer in some parts of the world) on account of our loyalty to the Torah, we are proud and grateful to G-d for having chosen us to receive the Torah. But this pride and gratitude must be tempered with humility and with the acknowledgement that it is for His service that we have been singled out. We bless G-d for having given us the Torah "with His holiness." Together with the Torah goes holiness — a holy way of life; that is, a life in which everything we do is dedicated to G-d. It is not a life of ease, but a life of service. G-d demands of His people to be a "holy nation." Many a time the Torah stresses: "You shall be holy; for I, your G-d, am holy."[6]

Thus, in the few words that make up this short prayer, we bring up the *past* — Mosheh and the Ark; and the *future* — the day when all the earth will be filled with the knowledge of G-d. And the two are linked with the *present* — our dedication to the

---

5. Isaiah 2:2-3.
6. Leviticus 19:2.

Torah in our present-day life. It is with this thought of holiness that we take out the Torah from the Ark.

בריך שמי'
Brich Shmei

Brich Shmei, a deeply moving prayer, is written not in Hebrew, but in *Aramaic*, a language similar to Hebrew spoken in Babylon. In this language the *Gemara* (as distinct from the *Mishnah*) is written, as also certain holy books (like the *Zohar*) and several other prayers. The prayer of *Brich Shmei* is an old one. It is first found in the *Zohar*,[7] the holy book composed by Rabbi Shimon ben Yohai, which contains many secrets of the Torah. This great and saintly man lived some 1800 years ago. We remember him especially on Lag B'Omer, the day he passed away, when many thousands of Jews visit and pray at his tomb in Meron in the Upper Galilee, in the Holy Land.

It is stated in the *Zohar*: "Said Rabbi Shimon, 'When the Congregation takes out the Scroll of the Torah to read in it, the Heavenly Gates of Mercy are opened, and G-d's love is aroused. Then the following prayer should be said — *Brich Shmei*...'"

Thus we learn that the time of opening the Ark and taking out the Torah to read is a very special time, a time of Heavenly mercy and love, when our prayers are especially acceptable. For this reason also we intone at this time, on the Three Festivals, on *Rosh Hashanah* and *Yom Kippur*, the special prayer of *Shlosh esrei middot* (*HaShem, HaShem*)[9] — the Thirteen Attributes of G-d's mercy and the prayer of *Ribbono shel olam* (Master of the World).

Because this prayer is in Aramaic, not everybody knows what

---

7. *Zohar II, Vayakhel* 206b.
8. Ibid.
9. Exodus 34:6-7.

it is about. But many prayer books have a translation of it, and it would be well for everyone to be acquainted with it.

The prayer begins with the words "*Blessed is the Name of the Master of the World*," and then goes on in the second person, "*Blessed is Your Crown and Your place (of Glory)*."

Because this is a favorable time, we continue:

> *May Your pleasure be with Your people forever, and may You show Your right hand's redeeming power to Your people in Your Holy House. Grant us of the goodness of Your light, and accept our prayers in mercy.*

When we speak of G-d's "right hand," we mean G-d's might and power with which He protects us and redeems us from our enemies. When G-d let our *Bet Hamikdash* be destroyed, it is said, "He held back His right hand."[10] So here we pray that G-d show us once again His right hand and bring us salvation by rebuilding His Holy House, the *Bet Hamikdash*.

After this short prayer for our people as a whole, we continue with a personal prayer:

> *May it be Your will to prolong our life in goodness, and may I be counted among the righteous, that You may show me love, and protect me and all that are mine (in common) with Your people Israel.*
>
> *You are He who provides food for all and sustains all; You are He who rules over all; You are He who rules over kings, and kingship is Yours.*

We pray to G-d to *open* our heart to His Torah. There is an inborn love for the Torah in our heart, but very often our heart is closed, and the love remains buried there. We pray that G-d *open* our heart a little, so that our love flows over and we become conscious of it and make it grow and overflow into our whole life.

We pray to G-d to fulfill our heart's desire, but not *any* heart's desire; only such that is "for good." We do not know what is really good for us; sometimes we ask for things that are not good

---

10. *Eichah* 2:3.

for us. But G-d knows what is good for us, so we pray that He fulfill our heart's desires *for good*, for life and for peace. And "life" means to us more than just existence; Jews were always ready to sacrifice their lives, if they could not live the life that G-d commanded us to live, a life in accordance with Torah and Mitzvot. And "peace" also means more to us than the absence of war. It means true peace and *inner* harmony, which can be achieved only when the soul is master over the body, when our love for G-d and the Torah makes all contrary desires meaningless.

At the conclusion of this prayer the Scroll of the Torah is taken out of the Ark. Usually a member of the congregation is given the honor of opening the Ark and taking out the *Sefer Torah*. On certain occasions, when it is necessary to read two or three different portions, two scrolls, or even three, are taken from the Ark. For example, when Shabbat coincides with *Rosh Chodesh*, or on the major festivals, two Scrolls are taken out; on Shabbat *Rosh Chodesh* Chanukah, for instance, three Scrolls are taken out. In such a case, one or two additional members of the congregation are honored by following the *chazzan* carrying the Scrolls of the Torah to the *bimah*.

When the Sefer Torah is taken from the Ark, the person taking it out kisses it and hands it to the *chazzan*. The *chazzan* kisses it, too, and, holding it in his right arm and embracing it with his left, turns to face the congregation. In the meantime, the Ark is closed and the curtain (*Parochet*) drawn (in some congregations the Ark is closed only after the *chazzan* begins to move away from it). Then, if it is during the morning prayer of Shabbat or any of the major festivals, the *chazzan* chants three verses, but only the last is recited at other times when the Torah is read. The three verses are the following:

1. *Shema* — The familiar declaration of the Unity of G-d, "*Hear, O Israel, the L-rd is our G-d, the L-rd is One.*"[11]

---

11. Deuteronomy 6:4.

2. *Echad* — *"One is our G-d, great is our Master, holy* (on *Rosh Hashanah*, *Yom Kippur* and *Hoshana Rabba 'and awesome'* is added) *is His Name."*

3. *Gadlu* — *"Glorify G-d with me, and let us exalt His Name together."*[12]

When the Torah is taken from the Ark, it is, of course, a most appropriate time to declare our faith in the One G-d, for the Torah is also one and only, holy and eternal. The fact that the *chazzan*, who is our representative, makes this declaration while holding the Torah, and that we repeat it after him, is like declaring it on oath.

In the second verse we declare the three qualities of the same One G-d. He is *One*, just as He was One before Creation; *Great* — as our Creator and Master; *Holy* — for He is so removed and beyond our understanding, that we know of Him by "Name" only. We know and feel G-d's presence in ourselves and in nature, for G-d dwells *in* this world. But at the same time, we know only of His existence, for He is above all and dwells also *outside* this world, we cannot, therefore, truly understand G-d's essential nature; He is "out of this world."

The third verse is a natural conclusion to the two preceding declarations of faith. Being a call by the *chazzan* to join him in praising G-d, it is not repeated by the congregation, but the congregation responds with two appropriate verses. The first *"Lecha Hashem hagedulah"* (Unto You, O G-d, belongs Greatness...) is fittingly taken from the prayer of David,[13] which is part of our daily morning prayers (*Vayevarech David*). This is a very significant passage in that it contains the Seven Attributes of G-d: *Kindness* (here *Gedulah* is used as a synonym for *Chesed*), *Might, Beauty, Victory, Glory, Foundation* (here the two words *ki-chol* adding up to eighty, represent the word *Yesod*), and *Royalty*. Each of these is a different aspect through which

---

12. Psalms 34:4.
13. Chronicles I 29:11.

G-d reveals Himself in the Creation and in His relationship with His creatures.

When we praise G-d by these qualities, we are reminded that our soul, which is a "part" of G-d, also has corresponding seven qualities which we must apply in our relationship to G-d and our fellow men. We must act with *kindness*, sometimes with *might* (in the sense of restraint), most often with a combination of the two, which is the quality of *beauty*, and so on.

This significant verse, with which the congregation responds, is followed by a second verse, which is in direct response to the second part of verse 3 above: "Exalt the L-rd our G-d, and bow down towards His holy mountain, for Holy is the L-rd our G-d."[14]

The three verses mentioned above, as well as the two verses of response, all combine to form one theme: G-d is One, although He reveals Himself in different ways. If it is difficult for us to understand how G-d can be kind and mighty, and reveal Himself in other different ways, yet remain *one and the same, without change, before creating the world as after creating it* — it is because G-d is *Holy* and beyond our understanding. Yet, G-d, in His kindness, has revealed much about Himself in the Torah which He has given us, and especially in its *inner* meaning, which is revealed in the wisdom of the *Kabbalah* and *Chassidut* — a vast and sacred literature that opens the way to attain a higher level of loving and fearing G-d, and coming as close to Him as is humanly possible.

יקום פרקן
Yekum Purkan

Yekum Purkan ("May salvation come forth") is the prayer said on Shabbat after the reading of the Torah. It is one more

---

14. Psalms 99:9.

prayer in our Siddur that is not in Hebrew but in Aramaic, as are *Brich Shmei* and *Kaddish*.

Yekum Purkan was introduced into our prayers some fifteen hundred years ago in Babylon, soon after the completion of the Talmud. At that time the greatest Jewish center was in Babylon. As the Jews then spoke Aramaic, a sister language of Hebrew, the prayer was written in this language so that everybody should understand it.

Jewish life in Babylon flourished at that time. The Talmud was studied with great devotion and diligence in the great Yeshivot of Neharde'a, Sura and Pumbedita. The Jews enjoyed much freedom and independence, able to live their way of life as a separate community. They had the privilege of electing a descendant of the royal house of David as their representative before the Babylonian government. He was called "Resh Galuta" — Exilarch (i.e., Head of the Exile), for the Jews never forgot that they were in exile there. All the Jews respected him greatly, and accorded him almost royal honor. He was regarded with great honor also among the dignitaries and officials of the government. He had a great deal of influence and power, and very often was also an outstanding Torah scholar. However, the real spiritual leaders of the people were the heads of the great Babylonian yeshivot who, after the completion of the Talmud, were called *Rabbanan Seburai* and (later) *Geonim*.

The yeshivot were very large at that time, for the study of Torah and Talmud was the most desired thing in those days. The number of regular students reached into thousands. When Rav was the *Rosh Yeshivah* in Sura, there were 1200 students who were supported by him, and Rav Huna had 800 students who were maintained by the yeshivah. These were students on "scholarship," but there were, of course, many more who required no support. Rav Huna had thirteen assistants who interpreted his lectures to the students, each one in charge of a large group of students.

The *Rosh Yeshivah* was called (in Aramaic) *Resh Metivta.*

There were also head-teachers, called *Rashei Kala*, who presided over the annual assemblies that took place two months in the year, the so-called *Yarchei Kala*. These were the months of Adar and Elul, when students and scholars from far and near joined the regular students, to review and revise what they had studied during the other months of the year.

In addition there were also *Dayyanim* ("judges") who were members of the *Beth Din* (courts), before whom all disputes were brought for judgment and settlement. These were called *Dayyanei d'Bava* ("Judges at the Gates").

The prayer of *Yekum Purkan* mentions them all. And now that we are familiar with these names and functions, we will take a look at the prayer and see what it means:

> *May salvation come forth from heaven, with grace, loving-kindness, mercy, long life, ample sustenance, heavenly aid, health of body, higher enlightenment, living and healthy children, children that will not cease from, nor neglect, the words of the Torah — to our teachers and rabbis, the holy congregation, who are in the Land of Israel and in Babylon; to the heads of the* Kala *and to the heads of the Exile and to the heads of the academies and to the judges at the gates....*

We can see at once that this is a prayer for the spiritual and material well-being and happiness of the leaders of the people. And there is no happiness without the blessing of children — "living and healthy children" by which is meant (as the prayer explains) "children that will not cease from, nor neglect, the words of the Torah." Although the center of the Jewish people and of Jewish learning was in Babylon at that time, the Land of Israel is mentioned first, out of respect and love for the Holy Land; and although only Babylon is mentioned with it, it includes all the lands of the exile, wherever Jews lived.

But the prayer is not only for the rabbis and teachers, but also

> *For all their students and the students of their students, and all those who occupy themselves with the Torah.*

May the King of the universe bless them, prolong their lives, increase their days, lengthen their years; and may they be saved and delivered from all trouble and mishap.

May our Master in heaven be their support at all times and in all seasons, and let us say, Amen.

What is the meaning of *"increased"* days and *"lengthened"* years? The length of the day and of the year is fixed. There are no more than 24 hours in the day, and the years, too, are of the same duration for all. Yet, in a deeper sense, the real length of time is determined by what one puts into it. The person who uses only half his time to good advantage, and wastes the rest, has only "half" a day; his days and years are "short." We pray for *long* days and *long* years — days and years filled to capacity with the things that are everlasting, the Torah and Mitzvot and good deeds.

Although this prayer was composed some fifteen hundred years ago, it is still valid for our times, for we do have spiritual leaders, rabbis and scholars, heads of yeshivot and students. We say this beautiful prayer for them every Shabbat, for we realize that upon their welfare depends the welfare of our people as a whole. And as we pray for them, we are reminded of our obligation to support them and the yeshivot, for by supporting them and enabling them to devote all their time to the study of the Torah, we become their partners and have a share in the Torah which they learn. Thus we are also included among "all those who *occupy* themselves with the Torah."

There is also a second *Yekum Purkan*, immediately following the first. It is almost identical, except that the prayer is for the congregation: "To all this holy congregation, the old with the young, children and women." It should also be noticed that while in the first *Yekum Purkan* the *third* person is used ("bless *them*"), the second person ("bless *you*") is used now, inasmuch as everyone addresses himself directly to the congregation present in the synagogue. That is why the second *Yekum Purkan* is omitted when one prays at home.

מי שברך

Mi Sheberach

At a later date, after the introduction of *Yekum Purkan*, and for the benefit of those whose spoken language was no longer Aramaic, an additional prayer, in Hebrew, was introduced. It is similar in content to the *Yekum Purkan* prayers, and is entirely in behalf of the congregation and its members: men, women and children, particularly those members who support the congregation and are involved in communal activities. The text reads:

> *He who blessed our fathers, Abraham, Isaac and Jacob, may He bless this entire holy congregation, together with all the holy congregations: them and their wives, their sons and their daughters, and all that belongs to them; those who establish synagogues for prayer, and those who come there to pray; those who provide light for illumination, wine for* kiddush *and* havdalah, *food for wayfarers and charity for the needy; and all those who occupy themselves faithfully with communal needs — may the Holy One, blessed be He, give them their reward, remove from them all sickness, heal their entire body, pardon all their sins, and send blessing and success in all their endeavors, together with all Israel their brethren, and let us say, Amen.*

"*Together with all the holy congregations.*" It is a time-honored custom when reciting a prayer, or extending a prayerful wish, in behalf of a congregation or individual, not to leave them singled out, but to associate them with all the other congregations, or with all our brethren. This, first of all, reflects the spirit of unity of the Jewish people. But, at the same time, it makes it more auspicious for invoking G-d's loving-kindness, since in unity there is also the combined merits of all who are included in the prayer or blessing. This form is frequently found in the Siddur.

"*...light for illumination, and wine for* kiddush *and* havdalah." A house of prayer has, of course, various upkeep expenses, such as heating and lighting, as we. as expenses connected with the performance of certain customs in the congregation, such as *kiddush* and *havdalah* (where it is customary to recite them in the congregation). It is, obviously, a special *zechut* (merit) to contribute towards these needs, and the more affluent members usually vied for this privilege, especially the privileges of providing "light for illumination" and "wine for *kiddush* and *havdalah*." This gave rise to an ancient custom (which is still very much alive in many congregations — performed at the beginning of the year, usually on *Shabbat Bereishit*) to "auction off" the privileges of contributing the money for the requirements, along with certain other honors (such as opening the Ark for taking out the scrolls of Torah and returning them, being called up to *Maftir* and *Haftarah*, etc.).

From the text of the prayer it can be surmised that it was intended to be said by the *chazzan*, but it became customary for the entire congregation to recite it, following the *Yekum Purkan* prayer. But it is recited only in the synagogue (as indicated by the words, "bless this entire congregation") and not when one is praying at home.

ברכת החודש
BLESSING THE NEW MONTH

On the Shabbat before *Rosh Chodesh* (New Moon), a special prayer for the new month is recited before the Musaf service after the reading of the weekly portion of the Torah and Haftarah, following the prayer of *Yekum Purkan* and *Mi Sheberach*. The central point of this custom is to announce the day (or two days) of the week on which *Rosh Chodesh* will occur.

Before discussing this custom, it will be useful to review briefly its origin and the general system of our Jewish calendar, the *luach*.

Our *luach* is basically *lunar*, that is, the months of the year are reckoned according to the moon. The Hebrew word *chodesh* means both "month" and "moon." The word is derived from the Hebrew *chadash*, "new," because the moon renews itself (reappears) every month as a narrow crescent. This monthly reappearance of the moon is called *molad* — the "birth" of the moon. The Jewish month is the period of time from one *molad* to the next, which is a little more than 29½ days (29 days, 12 hours and 44 minutes). Since a calendar month must consist of complete days (it would be very inconvenient to have half a day belonging to the outgoing month and the second half to the incoming month, and, moreover, a complete Jewish day includes the *preceding* night), our calendar months invariably consist of 29 or 30 days. In the former instance, the month is called *chasser* (deficient), in the latter, *malle* (full).

The first day of the new month is called *Rosh Chodesh*, "head of the month." If the outgoing month is a "full" month, then both its 30th day and the day following it (the first day of the new month) are *Rosh Chodesh*.

The days of *Rosh Chodesh* in our *Luach* have been designated in the Torah among the festive days of the year, which are celebrated by special laws, customs and prayers (as in the case of

Shabbat and the festivals, though not on the same level of holiness).

The lunar year (12 months averaging 29½ days, 44 minutes each) contains 354 days plus 8 hours and 48 minutes. (Interestingly, the Hebrew word for year (שנה) has the numerical value of 355. Thus, the lunar year is about 11 days shorter than the solar year, which has 365 days. Does it matter? Very much. Our festivals have been dated in the Torah, each to be celebrated on a certain day, or days, of a specific month.[1] At the same time, the Torah requires that our festivals occur in their respective seasons of the year, (e.g., Passover in the spring month of Nissan, Succot in the autumn harvest month of Tishrei).[2] The seasons of year, however, are determined by the sun, not the moon. Therefore, a periodic adjustment is required to reconcile the difference between the lunar year and the solar year. Without an adjustment our festivals would "wander" from season to season, being pushed back by 11 days from year to year, with the spring festival (Pesach) eventually falling in the winter, and the harvest festival in the spring, and so on.

This adjustment consists of the addition of an extra month once in two or three years. The extra month is added before the month of Nissan, giving us two months of Adar, and making that year a *shanah me'uberet*, a leap year, consisting of 13 months. This makes certain that the spring festival will not wander off from its season, and all other festivals will automatically fall into line. (There are 7 leap years in the 19-year lunar cycle — *machzor katan*, because during this period about 209 days, or seven months, are accumulated as the deficiency of the lunar year from the solar. They are the 3rd, 6th, 8th, 11th, 14th, 17th and 19th year, of the lunar cycle.)

During the time of the *Bet Hamikdash* the authority of determining which months should be "full" and which "deficient," as

---

1. Exodus 23:15; Leviticus 23.
2. Exodus 23:16, Deuteronomy 16:1, 13.

well as which years should be leap years, was vested in the *Bet Din Hagadol* (High Court) in Jerusalem. The High Court in *Eretz Yisrael* continued to exercise this function also after the destruction of the *Bet Hamikdash*. However, as life in *Eretz Yisrael* became increasingly unsettled, Jews ever more dispersed, and communications more difficult, the Sages decided to establish and make available a perpetual *luach*, incorporating the astronomical calculations as well as the time-honored principles that served as the basis of our Jewish calendar since the time of Mosheh *Rabbeinu*.

Our present fixed calendar was introduced by the Sage Hillel the Second, about the year 4119 of Creation (about the year 358 of the Common Era). It is an ingenious and marvelous system that tells us the exact point in time when the *molad* of the moon takes place, when *Rosh Chodesh* occurs, when all our festivals and fast days begin and end, how many days each month has, how many months each year has, and so on.

Soon afterward, in the era of the *Geonim* [4349 (589 C.E.) — 4798 (1038 C.E.)], the custom of announcing the New Moon in the *shul*, on the Shabbat preceding it, was introduced, partly as a reminder of the *Kiddush HaChodesh* (Sanctification of the New Moon) by the High Court of old, but mainly to inform the public when the actual day, or two days, of *Rosh Chodesh* will occur.[3]

יהי רצון
Yehi Ratzon

In Ashkenazi congregations the blessing for the new month is preceded by the prayer *Yehi Ratzon*, which is an adaptation of the prayer that Rav (of Rav and Shmuel fame) used to recite at the conclusions of the daily *Amidah*.[4] Rav's original prayer made

---

3. *Abudraham. Magen AVraham*, 417:1.
4. *Berachot* 16b.

no mention of *Rosh Chodesh* at all, but the appropriate words were introduced to connect the prayer with *Rosh Chodesh*. Thus it begins with the words,

> *May it be Your will, L-rd our G-d and G-d of our fathers, to renew for us this (coming) month for good and for blessing.*

It then goes on to petition G-d to grant us

> *long life, a life of peace, a life of good, a life of blessing, a life of sustenance (parnassa), a life of bodily vigor, a life marked by fear of Heaven and fear of sin, a life free from shame and reproach, a life of wealth and honor, a life in which we have love of Torah and fear of heaven, a life in which G-d will fulfill our heart's desires for good. Amen Selah.*

This prayer has not been included in *Nusach Ari*, because of the general rule that one should not pray for personal needs on Shabbat.[5] The reason for this, our Sages explain, is that Shabbat is a holy day, dedicated exclusively to spiritual aspects of the soul, without being distracted by any thought of the material and physical aspects of everyday life. Praying for such things as sustenance and health and similar needs is in order on weekdays but is not in keeping with the spirit of Shabbat. Such prayers inevitably bring to mind some measure of sadness or anxiety that would mar the perfect rest and delight (*oneg*) of Shabbat, when a Jew is to have the feeling that "all his work has been done."

מי שעשה נסים
Mi She'asah Nissim

In *Nusach Ari*, the prayer for the new month begins with *Mi she'asah nissim* (which in *Nusach Ashkenazi* follows *Yehi Ratzon*).

---

5. *Yerushalmi Shabbat* 15:3; *Vayikra Rabbah* end of ch. 34.

However, as is customary in all congregations, it is preceded by an announcement as to the precise moment of the *molad* (the moon's reappearance in the sky), stating the day, a.m. or p.m., the hour, minute and fractions as the case may be.

After this announcement, the Reader takes the *Sefer Torah* in his arms, while the entire congregation rises to recite *Mi she'asah nissim* and to hear the Reader repeat it and then pronounce when *Rosh Chodesh* is. The custom for the whole congregation to stand while *Rosh Chodesh* is proclaimed is in memory of *Kiddush haChodesh* by the High Court of old which was performed standing.

Here is the text of the short prayer:

> *He who performed miracles for our fathers and redeemed them from slavery to freedom, may He redeem us speedily and gather our dispersed ones from the four corners of the earth, uniting all Israel; and let us say, Amen.*

This is followed by the pronouncement, first by the Reader and then by the whole congregation:

> Rosh Chodesh (name of month) *will be on* (day, or two days, of the week), *coming to us for good.*

The reference to the miracles and the redemption from slavery to freedom is of course in regard to the enslavement of our ancestors in Egypt and their miraculous deliverance.

The connection between the Blessing for the New Month and the Exodus from Egypt is in the fact that the Mitzvah of *Kiddush haChodesh* — the very first Mitzvah that our Jewish people received from G-d — was given to us while our people were still in Egypt, exactly two weeks before the Exodus. It was then that G-d designated the month of Nissan (the Month of *Geulah*) to be the "head of the months" (*Rosh Chadashim*), first of the months of the year.[6] It is therefore fitting that we should recall the origin

---

6. Exodus 12:1-2.

of the Mitzvah of *Kiddush haChodesh* before we announce *Rosh Chodesh* in the congregation. At the same time, we express our fervent prayer that G-d should deliver us from the present *galut* very soon, and gather our dispersed people from the four corners of the earth back into our Holy Land, then the Mitzvah of *Kiddush haChodesh* will be reinstated as in the days of old.

יחדשהו
Yechadshehu

The concluding prayer for the new month is as follows:

May the Holy One, blessed be He, renew it for us and for all His people, the House of Israel, for life and for peace, for gladness and for joy, for deliverance and for consolation, and let us say, Amen.

Here we pray to G-d that he should *renew* the coming month (*yechadshehu* — from the same root as *chodesh*, "month" or "moon") as He renews the moon each month: "for life and peace, gladness and joy," as well as "for deliverance and consolation," meaning, of course, the ultimate redemption through our righteous *Mashiach.*

Thus, the custom of blessing the new month, with the announcement of the *molad* preceding it, reminds us of the symbolic link between the destiny of our Jewish people with the moon. The moon has its periods of increasing and diminishing brightness. But even when it seems to be hidden in total darkness, it is certain to "renew" itself and grow brighter and brighter, until it attains its fullness. So too with our people Israel throughout our long history; we rose from the darkness of Egyptian bondage to the heights of freedom as a "kingdom of *Kohanim* (G-d's servants) and a Holy Nation."[7] We received the Torah at Mount Sinai, entered the Holy Land, built the *Bet*

---

7. Exodus 19:6.

Hamikdash, and were led by our kings and prophets. But it was never an even course. There was the *churban* (destruction) and exile, followed by the return to the Land of Israel and the second *Bet Hamikdash*, with periods of eclipse under Greek oppression followed by regained freedom under the chashmonaim. But we soon fell under Roman occupation and the second *churban*, resulting in the exile and dispersion of our people to all the four corners of the earth in what is known as *Galut Edom* — our present, darkest but last *galut*.

And so *Rosh Chodesh* brings us a message of "renewal" and true consolation: no matter how dark it may be outside, there is no reason for despair, since this very month, perhaps even tomorrow, may bring the true and everlasting *Geulah*.

אב הרחמים
Av Harachamim

Av Harachamim ("Father of Mercies") is a memorial prayer for the souls of our Jewish martyrs who sacrificed their lives *al kiddush HaShem*, for the sanctification of G-d's Name. It is recited — followed by *Ashrei* — before the Torah is returned to the Ark, prior to the *Musaf Amidah*.

This prayer is not found in the *Siddur* of the *Rambam*, nor in Abudraham and Sephardi *Siddurim*. It is believed to have been first instituted in Germany after the terrible massacres and destruction of Jewish communities in the Rhineland regions and other parts by the Crusaders during the first and second crusades (1096 and 1146). At first it was recited only on the Shabbat before Shavuot because it was during the days of *sefirah*, between Pesach and Shavu'ot, that the worst massacres took place. Later, this prayer was adopted by most congregations in Poland and eastern Europe, and it became the custom to recite it every Shabbat except when *Rosh Chodesh* was announced, excluding the Shabbat before *Rosh Chodesh* Sivan, when *Av Ha-*

rachamim is said even though *Rosh Chodesh* Sivan is blessed on it. Nor is *Av Harachamim* recited when Shabbat coincides with a special festive day, such as on Shabbat *Rosh Chodesh,* Shabbat Chanukah, etc.

The opening words of this prayer, addressed to the "Father of Mercies," is a declaration that although our Jewish people have suffered untold persecution and martyrdom at the hands of the nations of the world throughout the ages, it has not diminished our recognition that He is our Father and, indeed, our *Merciful* Father. We realize that our human reason is too limited to understand the ways of *G-d*, but we are certain that He is the essence of goodness and mercy.

At the same time we "remind" HaShem, so to speak, of His promise to avenge the blood of our martyrs — all those saintly and righteous men, women and children and holy communities who gave their lives for the sanctification of His Name. For they died only because they were Jews, innocent victims of hatred and cruelty. All those Jewish victims and entire Jewish communities that had been wiped out by the Crusaders on the way to free the Holy Land from Moslem rule, could have saved themselves by agreeing to convert to the religion of their attackers. In many cases all that was necessary was to make a verbal declaration. Yet they refused even that.

Of course, G-d does not need to be reminded of His oft-repeated promises — in Torah, in the Books of the Prophets and in the Holy Writings (T'NaCh) that He would judge and punish the nations and individuals who mistreat us. The real purpose of this prayer is to remind *ourselves*. Reminding ourselves that G-d will punish our tormentors, makes it easier for us to bear the pain. More importantly, remembering the courage and self-sacrifice of our ancestors gives us additional strength to remain steadfast in our loyalty and devotion to G-d and to His Torah and Mitzvot in the face of all adversity. Thus, in reminding ourselves that G-d is our Merciful Father and we are His beloved children, we find both comfort and strength.

מוסף לשבת
MUSAF AMIDAH FOR SHABBAT

It has been noted[1] that our daily prayers, as well as our Shabbat, *Rosh Chodesh*, and festival prayers correspond to the *korbanot* (offerings) in the *Bet Hamikdash* of old. Since on Shabbat, *Rosh Chodesh*, and on the festivals there were *additional* offerings (*musafim*) in the *Bet Hamikdash*, we have on these festive days a special "additional" *Amidah*, called *Musaf*.

The *Amidah* of Shabbat and Yom Tov begins and concludes with the same three blessings as any other *Amidah*. In between, however, unlike the *Amidah* of weekdays which has 13 blessings, it has only one (except the *Musaf Amidah* of Rosh Hashanah, which contains three blessings). This central blessing is referred to as *kedushat hayom* — "sanctity of the day" or "sacred theme of the day."

The central blessing or prayer of Shabbat *Musaf Amidah* begins with the words *Tikkanta Shabbat* — "You (G-d) have instituted the Shabbat." [In other *nuschaot*: *tikkanta* (תכנת) with the letter כ meaning "established" — "You (G-d) have established the Shabbat."] The prayer is composed in reverse alphabetical order, beginning with the last letter of the *aleph-bet* — *tav* — and ending with the first letter, *aleph*.

In our Holy Scriptures [e.g. *Mishlei* (Proverbs), *Tehillim* (Psalms), *Eichah* (Lamentations)] we have many examples of alphabetical texts. Some of them have been included in our Siddur, along with prayers, *piyyutim* and *selichot* in alphabetical order. The alphabetical order is more than just a poetic form; it has special signficance, our Sages observe, in that it reflects and encompasses the totality of all the 22 holy letters of our Holy Tongue in which G-d's Torah has been written and given to us.

---

1. *My Prayer*, Vol. I, introduction, p. 10.

Moreover, there is a significance also in whether the order is straight up, from the *aleph* to the *tav* (*aleph, bet, gimmel, dalet,* etc.), or straight down, in reverse, from the *tav* to the aleph (תשר״ק — TaShRak). In general, the first symbolizes a movement from man to G-d; the second from G-d to man. Though both are integral parts in our mutual relationship with G-d, there are times when one or the other direction is emphasized. Thus, there are times when the initiative should come "from below," that is, from the individual, in terms of repentance and good deeds; while sometimes the initiative comes "from above," as an act of pure Divine grace and kindness, in order to trigger a corresponding response on the part of the favored individual.

In light of the above, it can be seen why the TaShRaK order is the more appropriate one for the *Tikkanta Shabbat* prayer of the *Musaf Amidah*, since the gift of Shabbat is an act of Divine grace, the culmination of the whole creation order, which was "created through kindness."[2]

It is also explained[3] that the TaShRaK order of this prayer alludes to the final ingathering and redemption of our dispersed exiles, which will come about in the merit of Shabbat observance.

As for the content of *Tikkanta Shabbat*, it expresses our gratitude to G-d for having instituted the Shabbat, for taking pleasure in the special Shabbat service and also for making the Shabbat a unique source of blessing, so that

> *those who delight in it inherit everlasting honor; those who taste it merit eternal life; those who love its precepts choose greatness* (also in this world)...

"*Those who delight in it... those who taste it... those who love its precepts...*" These expressions allude to the famous prophecy of Isaiah, linking the final redemption of our people with the observance of Shabbat (as mentioned earlier):

---

2. Psalms 89:3.
3. *Orach Chayim*, sec. 284:1; *L'vush, ibid.*

*If you restrain your foot because of the Shabbat, from
pursuing your needs on My holy day; and call the Shabbat a delight* (oneg), *HaShem's holy day — the honored
one; and shall honor it (by) not following your own
ways, nor pursuing your own needs, or speaking vain
words — then you will delight in G-d, and I will cause
you to ride upon high places, and will feed you with the
heritage of your father Yaakov. The mouth of G-d has
spoken this.*[4]

The second part of *Tikkanta Shabbat* expresses our fervent
prayer that G-d should

*bring us up in joy to our land and plant us within its
borders*

so that we can resume the Divine service in a restored *Bet
Hamikdash*, with the daily and additional *musaf* offerings

*as prescribed for us in G-d's Torah through His servant
Mosheh —*

specifically, the *musaf* sacrifice of Shabbat. Here we quote the
text in the Torah that specifies these sacrifices, namely, two
yearling male lambs without blemish, with the attending *minchah* (meal offering) of two-tenths of an *ephah* mixed with oil,
and wine offering.

Our Sages noted that the *musaf* offerings of Shabbat are the
most meager ones among all the *musafim* — only two lambs and
two-tenths of an *ephah* of fine flour. They explained it by means
of a parable: A king treated his servants to his royal table and
served them two dishes (a reference to the double portion of
manna — lechem mishneh — in the wilderness). When he was
ready for his own meal, the servants asked him, "What shall we
serve you, our lord?" The king replied, "What is good for you is
also good enough for me — just two lambs and two tenths of
fine flour."[5]

---

4. Isaiah 58:13-14.
5. *Kol Bo*, end of sec. 37.

In a related parable our Sages tell us that the Shabbat "complained" to G-d that it had been given such a modest *musaf*. G-d answered that, on the contrary, this *musaf* was especially fitting for Shabbat, because everything connected with Shabbat is "double": *lechem mishneh*; *zachor* ("Remember") and *shamor* ("Keep"); *oneg* (delight) and *mechubad* (honored), etc. It is therefore fitting that the Shabbat *musaf* should consist of "two lambs" and "two-tenths."[6]

The rest of the *Amidah* (*Yismechu* and *Elokeinu*, followed by the three last blessings) is the same as in the Amidah of Friday night and Shabbat morning (with the omission of the words "a memorial to the world of creation" in *Yismechu*).

---

6. Commentary of *Baalei HaTosefot* on Numbers 28:9-10, quoting *Midrash Shochar Tov*.

מנחה לשבת
MINCHAH FOR SHABBAT

Like every *Minchah* prayer during the year, it is customary to say first *Ketoret*. These are the chapters from *Chumash* dealing with the daily sacrifice (a lamb in the morning and lamb in the afternoon) and with the offering of the *incense* (*ketoret*), likewise twice daily. To these are added sections from the Talmud which deal with the same subjects, and the prayer of Rabbi Nehunia ben Hakane (*ana b'koach*). All this and more is said also in the morning.

The *Minchah* prayer for Shabbat consists of three main parts: first, there is the prayer (or psalm) of *Ashrei*, followed by *Uva l'Zion* and *Half-Kaddish*. Then there is the Reading of the Torah. *Half-Kaddish* is said again before beginning the silent *Amidah*, which is repeated aloud by the *Chazzan*. The repititon is followed by the full *Kaddish* (with *Titkabel*) and *Aleinu. Ashrei, Shemone Esrei* (on most weekdays also *Tachnun*) and *Aleinu* are said in the weekday *Minchah. Uva l'Zion* is said during the morning prayer on weekdays, therefore it is not said during *Minchah.* But on *Shabbat* (and Yom Tov) we do not say *Uva l'Zion* in the morning, so we say it during *Minchah.*

One of the reasons we do not say *Uva l'Tzion* during the morning prayer on Shabbat and Yom Tov but leave it for *Minchah*, is that the morning prayers on these days are long enough.

The reading of the Torah during the *Minchah* of Shabbat is taken from the first portion of the weekly *Sidrah*, due to be read on the following Shabbat morning.

The central prayer of the *Amidah* is *Atah Echad.*

170

אתה אחד
Atah Echad

Atah Echad — "You are One" — is, in a sense, the conclusion of the central prayers of the previous *Amidot* of Shabbat: *Atah Kidashta* — on Friday night; *Yismach Mosheh* — on Shabbat morning; and *Tikkanta Shabbat* of the *Musaf* prayer. As the famous commentator on the Siddur, the *Abudraham*, observed, we have in all these prayers one theme of the bride and bridegroom relationship. Therefore, the prayer of *Atah Kidashta* symbolizes *Kiddushin* — betrothal; *Yismach Mosheh* — the joy of the bridegroom with his bride; the *Musaf* — the special, additional gifts of the bridegroom to the bride; and *Atah Echad* — symbolizing the loving and eternal union between our people, the Shabbat and G-d, each one of the three being "one" and unique, and all three being united into one. For this reason, and others as the *Zohar* explains, the *Minchah* prayer of Shabbat is an *eit ratzon* — a moment of especial Divine favor. As we say just before taking out the Torah, "But as for me, my prayer is unto You, O G-d, in a *favorable time*; O G-d, in the abundance of Your mercies, answer me in the truth of Your salvation."[1] The significance of this verse becomes even clearer when it is considered in the light of the preceding verse in the above psalm. There King David, the Sweet Singer of Israel, speaks of the drunkards and enemies of our people who sit in the gates and engage in gossip and evil talk about the Jews. The contrast between the scoffers in the street and the holy people engaged in prayer in the *shul*, speaks for itself.

> *Atah Echad* — *"You are One, and Your Name is One, and who is like unto Your people, one people on the earth."*

This is a very meaningful phrase. It reminds us of the familiar

---

1. Psalms 69:14.

phrase which is mentioned many times in the Siddur and is also the concluding phrase of *Aleinu* — "And G-d shall be King over all the earth — in that day shall G-d be One, and His Name One."[2] The Prophet Zechariah speaks of "That Day," — the day when *Mashiach* will come and G-d's Glory will be revealed to all, and all the people will recognize G-d's Kingdom on earth. At that time all the people will recognize that there is only One G-d, the Creator. For the time being, however, different people worship different gods, by different names; some people even think that Nature is a "god" by itself. But in truth there is only One G-d, as we Jews proclaim in the *Shema* ("Hear, O Israel, the L-rd is our G-d, the L-rd is One"). And during the *Minchah* of Shabbat, when we come so close to G-d that we can say to Him: "You," we again declare, here and now (what other people will see later — on "that day") that "You are One and Your Name is One."

And, because we are the only people and nation in the world that has declared G-d's absolute "unity," we are also one and unique — "one nation on the earth."[3] That word — *Ba'aretz* ("on the earth") — is meaningful, too, for while we are on this earth and engaged in "earthly" things, we are unique, for we recognize that the holy day of rest that G-d has given us is "the glory of greatness and the crown of salvation."

When we come closer to G-d through prayer and study of the Torah, Shabbat is to us

> *a rest of love and benevolence; a rest of truth and faith-fulness; a rest of peace, tranquility and security; a perfect rest, in which You take delight.*

The prayer *Atah Echad* concludes with the words:

> *May Your children recognize and know that their rest is from You and for the sake of their rest (the Shabbat) they will sanctify Your Name.*

---

2. *Zechariah* 14:9.
3. Samuel II 7:23.

Because the Shabbat comes once a week regularly, people are likely to take it for granted. It is necessary to *recognize* and to *know* that the Shabbat is from G-d, and what it means to our people as a whole, and to every Jew individually — our very life, peace and security. When the Jew realizes what the Shabbat means for him and his children, he is ready to make sacrifices for the Shabbat.

סדר הבדלה
HAVDALAH

Havdalah means "separation." It is the prayer that is recited over wine at the conclusion of the Shabbat.

The *Havdalah* comprises three parts. The first consists of joyful selections from Isaiah and Psalms, including also the famous verse from the Book of Esther: "*For the Jews there was light, joy, gladness and honor,*"[1] to which we add the words, "*so be it for us!*"

The middle part contains three blessings in this order: over wine, spices and light.

The concluding section begins and ends with the blessing praising G-d "*who separates between holy and profane.*" Four basic separations are noted in this *Havdalah* blessing, between holy and profane, between light and darkness, between Israel and the nations, and between the Seventh Day and the Six Days of Creation (workdays). All these separations find expression at the conclusion of Shabbat. We acknowledge and reaffirm them in the *Havdalah*.

Havdalah, however, means more than this. As Rabbi Samson Raphael Hirsch says: "The prayer of *Motzei Shabbat* (termination of Shabbat) tells us to carry the spirit of Shabbat into our weekday life, which means to preserve the sacredness of our Shabbat in our business and work throughout the week. Thus *Havdalah* teaches us to see the Almighty as the One Who created the light in the midst of darkness; Who made the Shabbat for us to experience the difference of a holy life. It is to remind us of G-d as the one Who made the order of the Seven-Day Week, making the seventh day a holy day, just as He made a division between light and darkness, between Israel and the other

---

1. Esther 8:16.

174

nations. The *Havdalah* reminds us that there is a separation between a holy and unholy life, and that we belong to the holy life."

Havdalah, like *Kiddush,*[2] is recited over wine. The significance of wine in connection with festive religious ceremonies has already been noted.[3] In regard to *Havdalah*, wine has a further significance in light of the general concept underlying the recital of Havdalah in terms of awareness of the division between the positive and negative, even where the line of demarcation may become blurred. We are reminded that while "wine gladdens the heart of man,"[4] it can also turn a man into an animal if taken in excessive quantity. For us wine is a Divine gift, and we recite a blessing over it on festive occasion. By using it as a means of our serving HaShem, we make it holy in the same way as the weekdays become holy when we conduct our everyday life in keeping with G-d's commands.

Following the blessing over wine is the blessing over spices, *Boray minay b'samim* — "(Blessed is G-d) Who creates various kinds of spices."

The main reason for the inclusion of the blessing over spices in the *Havdalah* will be understood in light of the natural properties of those vegetable substances we call "spices."

Spices may have little nutritional value, but they are highly valued for what they do to enhance the taste and quality of foods by means of their delicate flavors and aromas. Many spices are also used in the preparation of medicines. Fragrant spices not only provide pleasing smells to improve the air we breathe, but have a unique quality of relieving faintness and headaches. Such is the effect of smelling salts, for example, which are made of certain chemicals mixed with perfume.

---

2. See pp. 84ff. above.
3. See p. 85 above.
4. Psalms 104:15.

Now, as already noted,[5] our Sages declare[6] that on Shabbat we are imbued with an "additional and higher soul," a special Shabbat soul, so to speak, so that we can better receive and enjoy the great spiritual (and thereby also material) benefits of this special day. As Shabbat departs, this "additional soul" departs too, leaving us somewhat faint and saddened. For this reason we inhale the *soul-refreshing* fragrance of spices during *Havdalah*, reciting the appropriate blessing first, in order to feel spiritually invigorated and cheered.

Indeed, our Sages declare that the only sensory perception from which the soul can derive pleasure is that of fragrance.[7]

Incidently, the blessing over spices is an expression of our gratitude to HaShem for giving us the wonderful sense smell, and the opportunity to use it in serving Him with it, too.

Our Sages further tell us[8] that Shabbat itself is a secret "spice" that makes everything taste especially delicious that day. Thus we are symbolically reminded to retain and carry over some of the Shabbat inspiration and influence into the coming weekdays.

The third — and highly visible — element in the *Havdalah* is the *Havdalah* candle, over which we say the blessing *Boray m'oray ha-esh* — "(Blessed is G-d) Who creates the lights of fire."

It is customary to hold up the closed palm of one's right hand to the light of the *Havdalah* candle, with fingers folded over the thumb, and to look upon the four nails reflection the light of the candle. The reason for this procedure is that we must make some real use of the light when we recite the blessing over it.

The reason we make the blessing over the "lights of fire" at the termination of Shabbat is that it was on the night of the seventh day of Creation when Adam made the first artificial fire.

---

5. See pp. 48, 53, and 56 above.
6. *Taanit* 27b.
7. *Midrash Tadshe* (or *Braita dR. Pinchas ben Yair*), 11.
8. *Shabbat* 119b.

Our Sages tell us that when G-d created the first man, Adam, on the sixth day of Creation, darkness never descended on earth until the following night. When darkness finally came, Adam was frightened. By Divine Providence, he chanced upon two flints, which he struck one against the other and produced the first man-made light. Thereupon Adam recited the blessing *Boray m'oray ha-esh*.[9] Moreover, it is particularly meaningful to recite this blessing in the *Havdalah*, since throughout Shabbat we are not permitted to make a light, or make use of fire for cooking, baking, etc. Thus, it is only after *Havdalah* that we are permitted to resume these and other weekday activities.

The *Havdalah* candle consists of at least two candles, or tapers, braided together, so that the two wicks produce a double flame. This is designed to correspond to the text of the blessing in which the plural form — *m'oray ha-esh*, "lights of the fire" — is used, alluding to the fact that there is more than one source of light. There is also the allusion to the fact that there are many hues of color in the light of a flame: red, white, green, etc.[10]

At the same time there is a meaningful lesson in the double flame of the *Havdalah* light, a lesson similar to that of the wine, mentioned earlier, in terms of utilizing all things in a positive way, in keeping with the design and will of the Creator of all things.

Fire is a most precious tool that G-d has given to man by which to shape his life. It was only after the discovery of making and using artificial fire that human civilization began to develop. Used properly, as a source of light, heat, and energy, fire is one of G-d's greatest gifts to mankind; used carelessly, not to mention maliciously, fire could be man's worst enemy. Such earnest reflections might well come to mind as we look on our fingertips bathed by the glow of the *Havdalah* light, at the moment of reentry into the dull and, sometimes, dreary weekdays. The *Havdalah* light thus serves as a visible symbolic reminder that "for

9. *Pesachim* 54a; *Bereishit Rabbah* 11:2.
10. *Rav's Shulchan Aruch*, sec. 298. par. 4.

Jews there is light, joy, gladness and honor" — the light of Torah and joy of Mitzvot, which dispels all darkness and gloom, and turns night into bright daylight.

Thus we conclude our excursion into Shabbat prayer on the topic of light, highlighted also in the *Foreword*. We noted there that Shabbat is ushered in with light — with lighting the Shabbat candles, and is escorted out with light —. the light of the braided *Havdalah* candle. This is profoundly significant in view of the essential aspect of Shabbat being a living memorial to G-d's work of Creation. Indeed, Creation first came into being, *manifestly*, by the Divine fiat, "Let there be light!"

It will be recalled that in the language of the Kabbalah light is identified with the "Infinite Light" (*Or-Ein-Sof*) emanating from the Creator. Hence, the conception of the creative process in terms of light emanation. This metaphor is particularly fitting because physical light has no independent existence separate from its source. Similarly, the universe — the totality of all things that exist and any particle of it — having been created out of nothing, can have no existence independent of the Creator. In other words, Creation is not a one-time act, but a *continuous* process.

What is true of the entire created order that came into being during the six days of Creation, is true also of Shabbat, created on the seventh day and blessed and sanctified by the Creator. The Divine blessing and sanctification of Shabbat is likewise a continuous emanation from G-d, the Source of blessing and holiness.

In turn, Shabbat has been designated as the source of blessing for all the days of the week.

This is the Shabbat that has been given to our Jewish people — "the people who [know how to] keep the seventh day holy"[11] — because this is the people whom G-d designated at Sinai as "a kingdom of kohanim (G-d's servants) and a holy nation."[12]

---

11. *Shabbat Amidot* (except at *Minchah*).
12. Exodus 19:5.

INDEXES

Index I
Quotations and References

2. Midrashim

General Index